INSIGHT *Pocket* GUIDES

# ROME

APA PUBLICATIONS

*Dear Visitor!*

The Roman's Rome lies 4m (3ft 6") under the new one, visible only at the Forum. But that's only one of the two great empires this city has nurtured. The Rome of the Church has the Vatican and its fabulous museums, as well as more than 2,000 churches – Romanesque, Renaissance, baroque – and probably just as many palaces, built by people of secular as well as ecclesiastical power and fame.

In these pages, one of Insight's regular writers and editors, John Wilcock, and Rome correspondent Angelo Quattrocchi peel back the many layers of the Eternal City to help visitors get the most out of a week-long stay. Their guide divides into three sections: *Day Itineraries*, comprising four full-day tours focusing on the four key areas (the Centro Storico, the archaeological zone, the Vatican and Trastevere); *Pick & Mix*, seven shorter itineraries, appealing to a range of different tastes; and *Excursions*, four worthwhile excursions to towns and sights within easy reach of Rome.

**John Wilcock,** an internationally known journalist who blazed a career from his native Yorkshire through such publications as *The New York Times* and *Village Voice,* has travelled the world for Insight. He was pleased that *Insight Pocket Guide: Rome* should give him the chance to team up with **Angelo Quattrocchi,** a friend and former colleague. Quattrocchi began his career as a foreign correspondent for Italian newspapers during the 1960 and '70s, later branching into books, TV and radio, Quattrocchi now divides his time between Tuscany and Rome, and has also written books on Milan.

*Hans Höfer*
*Publisher, Insight Guides*

# C O N T E N T S

### Excursions

Four excursions that can be made to interesting sights outside Rome.

### Eating Out and Nightlife

### Practical Information

### Maps

*Pages 8/9:*
*Fanfare in Piazza*
*Quirinale*

## Hub of a World Empire

Everybody knows the legend about the founding of Rome – how the abandoned twin sons of the war god Mars were suckled by the She-wolf until found and nurtured by a poor shepherd and his wife. When the twins grew up, they traced the outlines of the city with a sacred plough and then quarrelled over it. Romulus killed his brother and gave the city his name.

There is even a date attributed to its founding – 21 April, 753BC – although the legends don't clarify what day of the week it was. Far-fetched as this may sound, the date has gained some credence, at least with archaeologists excavating the Palatine hill who say that

*The She-wolf*

the so-called 'huts of Romulus' date from about that era and probably belonged to Etruscan, Sabine and Latin settlers.

The 1st-century writer Livy, who produced 140 books under the rubric *History of Rome*, endorses the tale of Romulus who, he wrote, invited all the neighbouring tribes to a big festival so that all the women could be kidnapped. This 'Rape of the Sabine Women' was 'a marvellous story', in the opinion of Livy and a worthy complement to his thesis that 'if any nation deserves the privilege of claiming divine ancestry, that nation is our own.'

Gradually the city spread over the six surrounding hills: the Capitoline, Viminal, Esquiline, Caelian, Aventine and Quirinal.

Tarquinius, the first Etruscan king, was succeeded by several others before the Etruscans were sent packing with the defeat of Tarquinius Superbus early in the 6th century BC. With the beginning of a republic in 509BC, two consuls – elected annually – ran the community. This became a triumvirate (Pompey, Crassus and Julius Caesar) in 65BC following seven years of Pompey singlehand-

*Classic torso*

edly holding power. Next it was Caesar who assumed authority, but only for a year or two before he was murdered by his jealous colleagues. Caesar's dalliance with the young Egyptian queen, Cleopatra, his dominance and his inevitable assassination make one of history's most dramatic and oft-told tales. Shakespeare's version is probably the most famous. Here he portrays Cassius persuading Brutus to join the plot against Caesar:

'Why, man, he doth bestride the narrow world
Like a Colossus, and we petty men
Walk under his huge legs, and peep about
To find ourselves dishonourable graves.
Men at some time are masters of their fates:
The fault, dear Brutus, is not in our stars,
But in ourselves, that we are underlings.
Brutus and Caesar: what should be in that "Caesar"?
Why should that name be sounded more than yours?'

After the defeat and deaths of the conspirators and through the decade that followed, a second triumvirate comprising Caesar's nephew Octavian, along with Mark Antony and Lepidus (who had served as one of Caesar's generals) maintained control. But during that time and for a decade afterwards the Republic was racked with dissent and civil war. Cleopatra had a fling with Mark Antony, too; she had tasted power and liked it. But after Augustus – as Octavian now called himself – expropriated her fortune and defeated Antony at Actium, she killed herself.

Augustus's 41-year reign was a golden age during which an efficient civil service was set up, Rome's brilliant engineers built an infrastructure that was to last for hundreds of years (some of it until this day) and such writers as Ovid, Virgil and Livy were at work. After Augustus's death, he was deified by the Senate and

*Emperor Augustus*

*Emperor Nero*

shrines were set up throughout the Roman Empire.

There followed a succession of tyrannical emperors – Tiberius, Caligula, Claudius and Nero – before Vespasian (AD69–79) seized the reins and restored order to the tangled state. Besides being the inventor of the pay toilet (a novel way to collect taxes), he also built the Colosseum, the biggest entertainment complex of its time. 'Bread and circuses' was the judgment of Juvenal, the 1st-century poet, on the way the city's rulers kept the populace distracted from seeking to improve their lot in life.

The 18th-century historian Edward Gibbon described the period after Mark Antony's death as 'a revolution which will ever be remembered and is still felt by the nations of the earth'. Gibbon's multivolume *The History of The Decline and Fall of the Roman Empire* explains how the structure of this society gradually fell apart, exacerbated by the decision of Diocletian to split the empire in two and Constantine's subsequent decision to move the capital east to Byzantium, afterwards called Constantinople.

Diocletian (AD284–305) did give Christianity some credence, however, and after a short-lived attempt by Julian (361–3) to restore paganism, his successor, Theodosius, in 380, made Christianity the official religion, in an edict that was not revoked until late in the 20th century.

The Church, seeing a power vacuum created by the emperor's absence from Rome, sought temporal as well as spiritual authority but its grab for control was premature.

In successive centuries, different waves of barbarians invaded and sacked the city, despite some not always wise papal alliances. The last

*Pope Leo*

would-be Caesar was the Goth invader Totila who, after taking over the city in AD546, staged the final chariot races in the Circus Maximus three years later.

Pope Formosus (891–6) and the five popes who succeeded him

brought the papacy to a low point, and in medieval times Rome was bedevilled by invaders from outside and rent with internal strife. In 1200 the city became an independent commune under Arnaldo di Breschia, who tried unsuccessfully to bring back a Roman republic complete with consuls and a senate. He was overthrown, tortured and hanged.

With the consecration of Clement V at Lyon in 1305, the papacy was hijacked by the French and moved to Avignon, where it remained for the next 70 years.

Pilgrims had long been Rome's major source of revenue. As long ago as the 6th century Pope Gregory I, inventor of the Gregorian chant, had contemplated destroying Rome's antiquities 'to concentrate the minds of visitors on spiritual matters', and in 1350 the city devised the idea of 'Jubilee Years'. Despite Petrarch's assessment that Rome was 'a shapeless heap of ruins', pilgrims began flooding in at the rate of 5,000 a day.

## The Renaissance in Rome

In both the 15th and 16th centuries, the glory of ancient, imperial Rome once again became an inspiration for those who could afford the luxury of the patronage of art. Classical Rome became the mainspring of the Renaissance, many of whose artists and writers 'laboured to restore the vast ruins and broken buildings of antiquity [as well as] the texts of its literature', as James Bruce Ross and Mary Martin McLaughlin put it in *The Portable Renaissance Reader* (Penguin, 1968).

Many of the glorious palaces of Rome and Florence date from this era and, following the lead of his predecessors, Nicholas V (who began work on the Basilica of St Peter's) and Sixtus IV (who commissioned the Sistine Chapel) as well as Julius II (1503–13) supported the work of artists, including Raphael and Michelangelo. Suddenly, artists who had previously ranked alongside humble artisans were mingling with the aristocracy.

In the 16th century, Gianlorenzo Bernini and his rival Francesco Borromini, both darlings of the papacy, filled the city with sumptuous churches and palaces, statues and fountains to glorify the Holy See, leaving a timeless

*Pope Alexander VI*

legacy of magnificent art while helping to emphasise the disparity between the immense wealth and extravagance of the Church and the poverty of its parishioners.

The Church was rich but Italy itself was even richer and it had long been the envy of other European powers. With the traitorous assistance of Milan's rulers and the support of the fanatical Dominican friar Savonarola in Florence, the French King Charles V invaded Italy in 1495 and battled with Italian troops at the village of Fornovo.

'If the Italians had won at Fornovo,' wrote Luigi Barzini in *The Italians*, 'they would probably have discovered then the pride of being a united people.' But such a dream was still three centuries away and with defeat Italy emerged as a rich prize sought after by half the nations of Europe.

Spain emerged as the winner and once again it was the papacy

*Meeting with the Pope, by Carpaccio*

which was only too happy to endorse its victory: Pope Clement VII crowned Spain's Charles V as Holy Roman Emperor in 1530 and he and his descendants ruled Italy with a heavy hand for the next century and a half. Then it was Napoleon's turn.

'The French army comes to break your chains,' he declared. '...we make war as generous enemies and we have no quarrel save with tyrants who enslave you.' Defeating the papal forces at Ancona, Napoleon demanded money and artworks from the Vatican, took Pope Pius VI across the border into France and married off his sister Maria Pauline to Prince Camillo Borghese. The prince responded by selling the Borghese family's art treasures for 30 million francs, a bargain job-lot that formed the basis of the Louvre's art collection.

After Pope Pius VII stubbornly declined to cooperate with Napoleon, French troops once again occupied Rome in 1808, sending the pope into exile in Savona and later in Fontainebleu. He was not to return until six years later.

In 1820 the long struggle of the Risorgimento began: the rise of modern Italian nationalism and the unification of the Italian states. Such patriots as Giuseppe Garibaldi (1807–82) and Giuseppe Mazzini (1805–72) struggled to unite the disparate states. Mazzini,

*18th-century Rome*

founder of a movement called La Giovana Italia, proclaimed a Roman republic in 1849 but the French were not giving up quite so easily. Supported by Pope Pius IX they invaded Rome once again and remained until 1870.

Supporters of unification had proclaimed the birth of a kingdom of Italy, with Sardinia's ruler Victor Emmanuel III as king of Italy almost a decade before, with the pope and the papal state confined to a suburb, but it was not until 1870 that the French left and the king's troops finally entered the city.

The following year, however, in May 1871, parliament tried to make peace by passing the Law of Guarantees allowing the Church to retain the Vatican City. Pope Pius IX was having none of it. He refused to accept the law and for good measure excommunicated its authors. Italy entered World War I on the side of the Allies in 1915 but the stand-off between Church and State continued for another half-century until in 1929, under Mussolini's fascist regime, the Lateran Treaty was signed between the secular government and Cardinal Gaspari representing the Vatican. Under this treaty, the Church was indemnified for the loss of its rights, and it was given authority over about 110 acres (44 ha) of Vatican property, including the papal villa at Castel Gandolfo.

## World War II and its Aftermath

Mussolini took Italy into World War II on 9 June, 1940, when he felt confident that Germany would win. Hitler, at first ambivalent about Mussolini's value as an ally, came to believe him more of a liability. 'It is in fact quite obvious,' he grumbled, 'that our Italian alliance has been of more service to our enemies than to ourselves.'

Eventually the Nazi leader found it necessary to despatch the German army to occupy Rome, meeting resistance from an underground movement, which provoked ruthless reprisals. Thousands died, including 335 killed in a mass murder at the Regina Coeli prison,

*Mussolini salutes the crowds*

before the Germans withdrew. Mussolini was hanged by partisans in the north, where Hitler had installed him as a puppet governor.

For four decades after the war Rome was a mess, physically and spiritually. The notable feature of its shaky infrastructure was unrestricted jerry-building, and there was widespread political, commercial and criminal corruption. Even the papacy was not exempt from scandal and sudden death. (Pope John Paul I died after a month in office.)

Finally, in 1992 the start of an anti-corruption campaign known as *Mani Pulite* ('Clean Hands') resulted in the jailing of 1,000 businessmen and accusations against hundreds of politicians and industrialists. Despite a resurgence of terrorism the following year, instigated by alliances between the Mafia and supporters of the status quo, there were signs of a moral resurgence in public life. In January 1995 a Mani Pulite party was formed.

Meanwhile Rome is preparing a huge celebration for the year 2000 to mark the start of Christianity's third millennium. Up to 30 million pilgrims are expected to visit in the jubilee year, putting enormous pressure on Rome's infrastructure and traffic system, which are well below par for a European capital. At the same time there are demands to improve living conditions for the three-quarters of Rome's 2.8 million inhabitants who live in the grim suburbs, which in aesthetic terms are a million miles away from the breathtakingly lovely centre.

*Anti-terrorist march, 1993*

# Historical Highlights

**753BC** According to legend, Romulus founds Rome and becomes its first king.

**509** Fall of the seventh king, Tarquinius Superbus. End of Etruscan rule. Republic proclaimed.

**387** Gauls conquer Rome.

**312–308** Appius Claudius builds the Appian Way.

**241** Victory in the First Punic War: Sicily becomes a Roman province.

**218** Second Punic War; Hannibal crosses the Alps.

**216** Defeat at Cannae; Hannibal *ante portas* (before the gates).

**202** Decisive victory over Hannibal in Battle of Zama ends war.

**146** Destruction of Carthage and Corinth.

**133** Civil war starts with the murder of Tiberius Gracchus.

**101** First clash with the Germans; Cimberi and Teutons wiped out.

**71** Gladiatorial War led by Spartacus ends in bloodbath.

**60** First triumvirate: Caesar, Pompey, Crassus.

**51** Caesar accomplishes his conquest of Gaul.

**44** Caesar assassinated.

**43** Second triumvirate: Antony, Octavian, Aemilius Lepidus.

**31** Caesar Octavian Augustus assumes autocracy.

**9** Danube border established.

**AD64** First persecution of Christians under Emperor Nero.

**98** Trajan takes up office. The Empire is extended.

**270** Aurelian builds a defensive wall round Rome.

**286** Diocletian divides Empire's administration into east and west.

**330** Constantinople becomes capital of the Empire.

**410** Alarich, leader of the West Goths, plunders Rome.

**452** Pope Leo the Great prevents Attila from conquering Rome.

**546** Totila, king of the East Goths, conquers Rome.

**800** Coronation of Charlemagne as Roman Emperor.

**1144** Arnaldo di Breschia tries – like Cola di Rienzo later – to separate Rome from the papacy.

**1300** Boniface VIII organises the first 'Holy Year'. Papacy at the height of its power.

**1309** Clement V chooses Avignon as his residence. Papacy falls under the influence of French kings.

**1378** The 'Avignon exile' ends with the election of Urban VI of Rome. Clement VII sets up as counter-pope.

**1417** The election of Martin V ends 40 years of schism; the pope is once again ruler of Rome.

**1527** *Sacco di Roma*: German and Spanish mercenaries plunder the city for months, 30,000 die.

**1572** Gregory XIII begins restoration of ancient water pipes; the Roman fountain tradition begins.

**1797** General Duphot raises the 'Roman Republic'.

**1815** The Roman Church State is restored by Congress of Vienna.

**1860** A large part of the Church State falls to the kingdom of Italy.

**1870** Rome, population 20,000, is conquered by Spanish troops and becomes capital of Italy.

**1922** Fascists march on Rome. Mussolini becomes dictator.

**1944** Allied troops march in to the city on 4 July.

**1957** The Treaty of Rome is signed on 25 March, laying the foundation for a united Europe.

**1994** Alliance between socialists and Christian Democrats which had ruled for 30 years is defeated by the 'Clean Hands' movement.

**2000** Rome will celebrate the start of Christianity's third millennium.

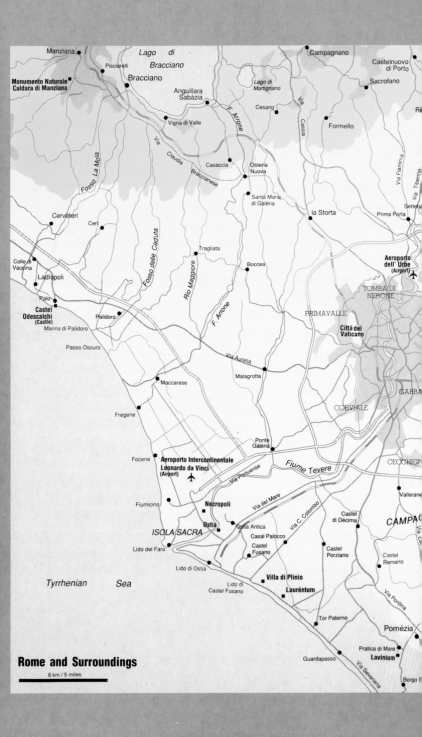

Rome and Surroundings

8 km / 5 miles

# Day Itineraries

The city of Rome, almost 4,000 years old, is really two cities: the centre and the suburbs. The centre comprises palaces, churches, piazzas, *viali* (tree-lined avenues) on what is left of the seven hills (one topped by a Hilton hotel). Big *portas* (arches) open into the famous Roman roads: the Aurelia, north to the sea; the Cassia, north to Viterbo and Florence; the Flaminia, north to Umbria; the Salaria, northeast to Abruzzi. The Tiburtina runs south to Tivoli and the hills called Castelli; the Tuscolana and the Appia Antica, south to Naples. The Tiber, bisecting the city, runs 24km (15 miles) west to the port of Ostia.

The itineraries section of this guide is split into three. The first, Day Itineraries, focuses on the main sights of ancient Rome, medieval Rome and Renaissance Rome and aims to capture the essential flavour of the city. The second, Pick & Mix itineraries, covers other interesting aspects and areas of the city, while a third, Excursions, suggests visits to towns and villages near Rome.

Don't make the mistake of trying to cram everything into a couple of days; Rome needs at least a week. It is probably the most engaging time-trip you'll ever have, so what's a week in Rome when she (and Rome is a she, of course) has been waiting for you for more than 20 centuries?

***From the dome of St Peter's***

DAY 1

**Start in Piazza Navona, visit lovely churches and the Pantheon, admire Bernini sculptures and a painting by Caravaggio, see the Trevi Fountain, the Spanish Steps and the Villa Borghese and end the tour in the Piazza del Popolo.** *See map on pages 18–19.*

Although what is now the **Piazza Navona** was built in the 1st century by the Emperor Domitian as a tràck for chariot racing (the losers were sometimes executed) it retains only its original shape – enhanced by the baroque buildings that surround it. The piazza's centrepiece is the magnificent **Fountain of the Rivers** whose meticulous sculptures by papal favourite Gianlorenzo Bernini (1598–1680) represent the Danube, Rio de la Plata, Ganges and the Nile. Its source at that time still unknown, the Nile has a head symbolically veiled, an upraised hand pointing to the church of **Sant' Agnese** built seven years later by Bernini's rival, Francesco Borromini.

When, in 1651, the fountain was unveiled, not a drop of water was to be seen and a dejected Pope Innocent X (whose coat of arms it bears) began to walk away. Only then did Bernini dramatically begin the flow. The pope turned back beaming happily.

Pigeons, souvenir salesmen ('your name on a grain of rice'), artists and tourists alike find the fountain irresistible and the piazza's extravagantly expensive restaurants are usually crowded. One can usually eat for half the price at cafés in the neighbouring streets.

Opposite the fountain at the piazza's southern end (its sea god an addition by Bernini) exit via di Lorenesi, crossing Anima to enter **Santa Maria dell' Anima,** the German national church (ring the bell), at the rear. The dimly-lit interior is a treasure trove of glorious frescoes, the one behind the altar by Giuliano Romano, a pupil of Raphael's. A famous painting by the master himself, *Four*

*Fontana Quattro Fiumi*

21

*House detail, Piazza Navona*

*Sybils*, sits in the adjoining **Santa Maria della Pace** but lately this has been closed for restoration. In this warren of quiet back-streets are innumerable antique stores and cafés, the best-known of which, the ivy-covered **Caffè della Pace**, has no sign. At No 9 Via della Rosetta is one of the city's best fish restaurants.

Adjoining Sant' Agnese church on the piazza is the **Palazzo Pamphili** (Pamphili Palace), now the Brazilian embassy, which owes its origin to Pope Innocent X, a member of the Pamphili family whose name also adorns the gorgeous villa and gardens behind the Gianicolo. The palace contains a gallery built by Borromini.

A famous resident of the palace was the pope's sister-in-law, Olympia, whose unpopularity around the Rome of her day was reflected in graffiti adorning the **Pasquino statue** on the corner opposite the building. Pasquino, a local shoe-maker who was no respecter of the all-embracing Church, established the custom of attaching anti-papal messages to the old marble statue (its Hellenistic origins are uncertain) and the practice continued through the centuries.

Leaving Navona from the side opposite the church, you are confronted by the 400-year-old **Madama Palace**, built for the Medici family, two of whose members became popes. It was named for Margarethe of Austria, bastard daughter of Charles V, who married first Alessandro de' Medici and then, on his death, Ottavio

*The Pantheon*

Farnese. As a consequence of this liaison the fabulous Medici art collection was split between the two dynastic families. One block right along the Corso del Rinascimento at the Archivo diStato sign, pass through the courtyard, pausing to admire Borromino's twisted spire on the church of **Sant' Ivo** (usually closed), leaving via the dark alley on the right. Two blocks left along Via Dogana Vecchia is the church of **San Luigi dei Francesi**, with works by Caravaggio in the fifth chapel on the right. Brawler, gambler and convicted killer, Caravaggio (1573–1610) was also one of the great painters and his admirers are legion.

Across the street a sign points along Via Giustiniani to the **Pantheon** (open mornings only), the best-preserved of all Roman temples despite being continually gutted by several popes. Urban VIII, for example, melted down its bronze girders to make cannons.

The structure, built during the reign of Hadrian (AD118–125) in place of an earlier temple by Agrippa, is still uniquely impressive with its 43.3-m (140-ft) wide dome so high that the circle of light at the top seems scarcely bigger than a rabbit hole. When Raphael died in 1520 his request to be buried here was granted.

The street along the Pantheon's south side leads past the Bernini-designed elephant topped with an obelisk, to **Santa Maria Sopra Minerva** whose many famous tombs include those of two Medici popes and the Dominican monk Fra Angelico whose 15th-century art is renowned for its bright colours and matchless piety. Near the altar are frescoes by the Renaissance painter Filippino Lippi, and a statue by Michelangelo.

Back to the Pantheon where, just beyond, the cheerful pizzeria **La Maddalena** is an inexpensive spot for lunch. Afterwards, continue along Via Maddalena, turning right along Uffici del Vicario, past the famous ice-cream parlour **Giolotti** and into Piazza dei Montecitorio. The buildings here and in the adjoining Piazza Colonna are those of the Italian Parliament and Senate.

The startling **Column of Marcus Aurelius** is engraved with reliefs depicting the 2nd-century emperor's military campaigns. Restored in 1588, its interior contains a spiral staircase (no longer used).

After crossing the Corso en route to the Fontana di Trevi turn one block to the right to admire the venerable **Sciarra Gallery** with its bizarre mix of architectural styles.

The **Trevi Fountain**, one of Rome's most popular sights, was built in 1736 and funnels water from an aqueduct more than 2,000 years old. In Fellini's *La Dolce Vita*, Anita Ekberg used it for a midnight bath and everybody knows that to throw a coin into it is to ensure your return to Rome. Not long ago, the owners of the

*Sunny day on the Spanish Steps*

*In the grounds of Villa Borghese*

building housing the Hotel Fontana were offering to sell the ground floor for a mere £8 million. Another famous landmark, the **Piazza di Spagna**, is about 20 minutes' walk from here, along Lavatore to Due Macelli. In summer the Spanish Steps are lined with flowers but they're crowded at any time of the year. Many come here to patronise American Express or McDonald's. The quaint English tea-room, **Babington's**, charges L26,000 for Welsh rarebit with even a Coca-Cola costing the equivalent of about £4.

Three parallel streets running off from the piazza – Frattina, Condotti and Borgognona – attract Rome's smartest shoppers with such famous names as Armani, Gucci, Bulgari and Cartier.

*Detail, Santa Maria del Popolo*

At the top of the Spanish Steps, and to the left is the **Villa Medici** built atop the one-time Gardens of Lucullus. It is now the French Academy, whose students have included Berlioz, Debussy and Fragonard. The fountain was sketched by Goethe in 1787. At the very top of the incline, in the park of the **Villa Borghese**, is a favoured eating place of visiting dignitaries, the **Casina Valadier**, surrounded by busts of statesmen, artists and writers.

It was the architect Giuseppe Valadier who laid out the impressive **Piazza del Popolo** below. In the centre is an Egyptian obelisk which Augustus originally had installed in the Circus Maximus. The Via del Corso ends here in red-brick walls 25m (82ft) high, marking the boundary of the ancient city. The Corso runs across Rome in a straight line to Mussolini's hideous Monument to Victor Emmanuel, which Romans deride as *La Machina Escrivere* ('the typewriter'). At the station across from the Piazza del Popolo you can take a train north to medieval Viterbo (2½ hours), the home of the pope in the 13th century, or stop off at such charming villages as Sacropano or Soriano del Cimino.

## Ancient Rome

**Where the city began on and below the Palatine hill; Michelangelo's piazza and the Capitoline museums; plus the Forum, Colosseum and Circus Maximus.**

Surrounded by buildings and statues by Michelangelo, there's no better place to start exploring ancient Rome than the **Campidoglio** – then, as now, the seat of the city's government. Here stood the immense bronze statue of Marcus Aurelius which is now protected from pollution behind glass in the courtyard to your left. The corridors of the **Palazzo del Museo Capitolino** are lined with statues and busts, some of them of mythical figures such as Bacchus, Cupid and Psyche, others of prominent Romans of the day. A justly famous piece is the *Red Faun*, a rosy marble version of the Greek original that belonged to Emperor Hadrian, who built

*Piazza del Campidoglio*

the villa at Tivoli and was closest to the Greek civilisation.

At a mere 50m (64ft) in height, the Capitoline is the lowest of Rome's seven hills and the Campidoglio (simply the Italian word for 'Capitol') which stands on it was once a sacred sanctuary called the Asylum where the persecuted could take refuge.

The **Palazzo dei Conservatori**, on the right, deserves more time for it contains many masterpieces, among them the Etruscan She-wolf suckling Romulus and Remus and the 1st-century sculpture of a boy taking a thorn out of his foot. Stretching right up to the 12¼-m (40-ft) ceiling of one room, a mural records the days when battling tribes sometimes settled their disputes by choosing gladiators to represent them. On this occasion, with two Romans killed, the third ran fast enough to outpace his rivals, turning to kill them one by one.

Upstairs, in the first room, note the lovely *Portrait of a Young Woman* by Domenico Paneoti (c 1480) and, in the next room, *Portrait of a Young Man* by

*Bronze of Marcus Aurelius*

Giovanni Bellini, the dominant Venetian painter of the 15th century. Tintoretto and Bassano are also represented in this room, as is Paolo Calliani (1528–88) with his *Rape of Europa.* Reni's self-portrait adjoins the large painting of Romulus and Remus by Peter Paul Rubens (1577–1640).

Turn right as you leave the museums and walk down Via del Campidoglio, past the town hall, for an overview of the **Forum.** Over to the left is the **Arch of Septimius Severus**, which in AD203 celebrated the first decade of the reluctant emperor's reign. Nearby eight pillars remain of the **Temple of Saturn**, which sheltered the state treasury, and three pillars of the **Temple of Vespasian** (who built the Colosseum). It was the custom of generals and emperors to erect columns and arches to celebrate their victories and, beginning with Caesar, some built entire new forums. There was a tendency for the populace to regard emperors as gods when they died and this was certainly the case with Caesar to whom Augustus erected a temple. It stood, and still stands, on the spot where he was cre-

*Forum Romanum*

mated after his assassination in 44BC. Augustus himself became a god-like figure during his 41-year reign, assuming the title of Pontifex Maximus afterwards adopted by the popes.

Later, Cleopatra's wealth was expropriated by Augustus who used it to transform Rome from 'a city of brick into a city of marble' – the city you see before you in the Forum. Even centuries of neglect, followed by the wholesale plundering by Renaissance ar-

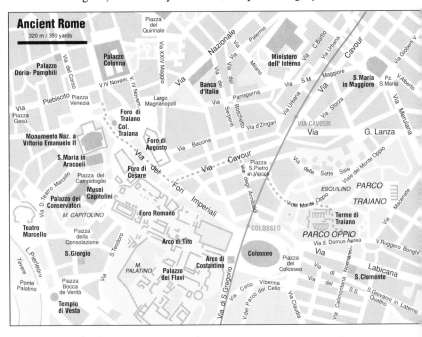

*Constantine II sculptures*

chitects, who dismantled entire buildings to incorporate the materials into their palaces, has not diminished its majesty.

Close to Caesar's temple is one devoted to **Vesta**, goddess of the hearth and patron of the state. Chosen from good families with impeccable pedigrees, the ladies who became Vestal virgins watched over a sacred image of Minerva (daughter of Jupiter and Juno) and kept the sacred flame alight through wind and storm. They served a term of 30 years and were obliged to remain inviolate on pain of death (their lovers were strangled). In return for their faithful service they were honoured everywhere, travelling in wheeled carriages and favoured with the best seats on all public occasions.

Next to the **Temple of Castor and Pollux,** twin sons of Jupiter, is the **Temple of Caesar**. Other notable structures include the **Basilica of Constantine**, about halfway up the left-hand side, where a colossal statue was found in 1487. Long ago broken up, its hands and feet stand in the courtyard of the museum. At the far end, near the rebuilt **Arch of Titus**, are the extensive ruins of *Vestal virgin* the **Temple of Venus and Rome** designed by Hadrian in AD125, destroyed by fire in 307 and rebuilt by Maxentius. Up the hill to the right from where you stand is the **Tarpeian Rock**, named for the 8th-century BC traitor Tarpeia who let the besieging Sabines, led by her lover King Titus Tatius, into Rome (they were swiftly ejected and Tarpeia herself was crushed to death between the soldiers' shields). Traitors were subsequently tossed from this rock.

Head back out of the piazza and down the stairway. Viewed from across the street, the two sets of side-by-side stairways are an impressive sight but the 125 wide marble steps leading up to the Aracoeli church are steeper and higher. They were built in the 14th century, when the church was already 100 years old, and according to legend bring good fortune to the buyer of a lottery ticket who is willing to climb them on his/her knees. **Santa Maria in Aracoeli**, at the top, sits on the site of a temple to Juno where Augustus later built an altar.

Juno's full name was Jupiter Moneda, whence comes our word money because her temple was also the site of the earliest mint. Geese were sacred to Juno and their honking is said to have warned the Romans of an attack by the Gauls in 390BC. The church contains Pinturicchio paintings of scenes from the life of Siena's St Bernardino.

The **Via dei Fori Imperiali** leading beyond the Colosseum to the Appian Way, the major route to the south, was constructed by Mussolini who cleared acres of ruins to build it. Il Duce was in a big hurry to demonstrate the results of his ambitious plans so apparently lacked the patience to investigate what could have been a treasure-trove of antiquity. Thousands of people were evicted to make way for the grandiose project. With them went what was left of innumerable temples, arches and palaces.

At the far side of the broad street are the forums built by Augustus, Caesar and Nerva, the emperor who in AD96 succeeded Domitian but whose rule lasted for a mere two years. Here also are the astonishing markets of Nerva's successor, Trajan, who in AD106 hired the best architect of his time, Apollodorus of Damascus, to create what was in effect a 2nd-century mall offering one-stop shopping. At the eastern end of **Trajan's Market** is a huge Renaissance palace that, though built 1,300 years later, blends perfectly because, of course, the Renaissance was inspired by classical Rome whose aesthetic it strove to reproduce.

Living on the plunder of the empire and spending money freely, the imperial rulers kept the masses distracted on a diet of 'bread and circuses'. In the **Colosseum** 55,000 spectators could be entertained at once. The Colosseum stands on the site of what was Nero's artificial lake, 188m (617ft) long by 156m (512 ft) wide and opened in AD80 with three months of games. Christians reputedly fought lions, gladiators fought each other and wounded contestants lived or died according to the emperor's whim, expressed by thumbs pointing up or down. Volunteer gladiators were rare; they were usually prisoners or slaves who along with the animals waited their turn in the warren of rooms and corridors beneath the arena.

As founder of the Colosseum, Vespasian (AD69–79) was the Broadway impresario or P T Barnum of his time, and, succeeding Nero (whose excesses had led to his involuntary suicide), he chose for his site part of his predecessor's estate. As late as the 16th century, relics of the Nero era were still turning up on his former property. The long-sought Laocoon statue (now in the Vatican museum) was discovered here – 1,200 years after Pliny the Elder first catalogued it.

The **Palatine**, which can also be

*Temple of Caesar*

*The Colosseum*

reached via the Arch of Titus in the Forum, was the roosting place of many famous men: Catullus and Cicero, as well as the emperors Augustus, Tiberius, Caligula, Nero, Domitian and Septimius Severus all built homes here, and were nurtured by a temple to the moon goddess Cybele. 'We honour men by speaking, the gods by silence,' wrote Plutarch, possibly referring to the no-talking rule observed in Cybele's temple.

Just east of the (headless) statue of Cybele and behind the remains of the **Temple of Apollo** was the house of Augustus and his wife Livia with frescoes that have

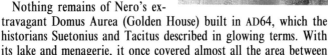

been dated to around that emperor's time. According to the biographer Suetonius, the original house was a modest one in which Augustus lived simply for 40 years. Rooms were added gradually but appear to have been used mostly for public functions.

Nothing remains of Nero's extravagant Domus Aurea (Golden House) built in AD64, which the historians Suetonius and Tacitus described in glowing terms. With its lake and menagerie, it once covered almost all the area between the Palatine and Oppian hills.

The biggest palace on the Palatine was that of Domitian (whose Arch of Titus in the Forum honoured both his brother and his father Vespasian. The public wing, **Domus Flavia**, became the main imperial palace for the next three centuries and even today its surviving walls are impressive. Domitian's living-quarters were in the other wing, the **Domus Augustana**, where despite his somewhat paranoid precautions he was assassinated in AD96. The immense **stadium** dates from about the same period. The other major attraction on the Palatine hill is probably the **botanical garden** which

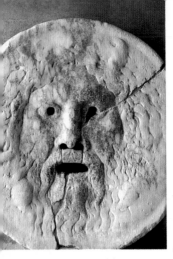

*Bocca della Verità*

Pope Paul III's grandson, Cardinal Farnese, built in the mid-1500s over the ruins of Tiberius's palace.

Between the Palatine and Aventine hills is the empty, open space of the **Circus Maximus** which is said to have been constructed as early as the 7th century BC but achieved much of its fame from the mock battles and chariot races of the era beginning with Julius Caesar. The long, grassy hollow, banked at one side, hasn't seen a chariot race since AD549 and today is a traffic-free way to walk between the Palatine and the circular **Temple of Hercules**. With its distinctive pillars, this is the oldest marble building in the city. Close by is the rectangular 1st-century BC **Temple of Portunus,** god of rivers and ports. Collectively these temples near to the Tiber are known as the Forum Boarium, the name referring to the cattle market that once stood here when this area was the site of Rome's first river port.

Just across the street, **Bocca della Verità** ('the mouth of truth'), a stone head, sits in the foyer of **Santa Maria in Cosmedin** church, an irresistible lure for tourists who like to photograph each other inserting their hands – which, legend avers, will be bitten off if they tell a lie.

If you head up along the river to finish this tour beside the **Fabricio** bridge which crosses over to the island of Tiberina, you'll see to the right the massive walls of the **Theatre of Marcellus** whose massive curved wall features in a famous 19th-century print by Thomas Hartley Cromek, much reproduced on postcards.

Marcellus was the nephew of the emperor Augustus who dedicated the theatre to him after his early death while still in his teens. It was said to have been a model for the Colosseum but much of the original theatre has been subsumed into the 16th-century palace built by Baldassare Peruzzi for the Orsini family.

*Via del Teatro Marcello*

## Trastevere

**A casual stroll through Rome's 'Bohemian quarter' beginning at the Sisto bridge, checking out some recommended restaurants and (on Sundays) the flea market. The day ends with a far-reaching view from the Gianicolo hill.** *See map on pages 18–19.*

For many visitors Trastevere is the most colourful part of the city. Meandering from the Tiber's 'Left Bank' to the Gianicolo it has become the equivalent of New York's Greenwich Village or London's Soho. And naturally the presence of artists and writers has attracted a predictable influx of jewellery and leather stores, cute bistros and a volume of musical night-life, but on the whole Trastevere ('across the Tiber') has remained remarkably unspoiled. This is still the lived-in neighbourhood it has been for centuries. Mingled with people choosing alternative life-styles, are born-and-bred locals who have never crossed the Tiber in their entire life.

*View from the Acqua Paola*

Beginning at the **Ponte Sisto**, descend the steps to admire the **Acqua Paola** fountain, its inscription crediting Pope Pius VIII with providing water to bring his flock 'cleanliness and joy'. (Among Pius's other good works, incidentally, was the launch of the efficient Vatican postal service).

The flood-barrier walls were built by Mussolini in the 1930s, their unforeseen side-effect being to prevent navigation, although every July a solitary tourist boat sails from Ponte Garibaldi – the next bridge down – all the way to the sea at Ostia. Until the embankments were built in the last century, there were still traces of the old port, the Ripa Romea, where Vatican-bound pilgrims arrived by boat.

**Tiber Island**, reached by the Ponte Fabricio built in 62BC at one side and the Ponte Cestio (built 20 years later) at the other, is boat-shaped and is the only one in the river. It is mostly taken up by a hospital and has been associated with healing since, legend relates, Asclepius sent a boatload of magical snakes to the island to cure a plague (*see page 58*). By the river on the Trastevere side the high embankment offers a delightful place to relax, sitting with one's back to the wall when the sun is high in the sky.

**Viale di Trastevere**, the main road through the district, begins at the Garibaldi bridge. To the left of the lifesize statue of Giuseppe Belli, the 19th-century author of hundreds of satirical stanzas in the Roman dialect, is the medieval **Torre degli Anguillara**.

On Sunday mornings continue along the Viale for about seven blocks, turning left into the flea market when you see the stalls. It covers an enormous area all the way back down to the **Porta Portese** by the Subicio bridge. To the right are stalls selling clothing of the type found anywhere, but the left flank is more interesting, with everything from stuffed mooseheads and stained-glass windows to toilet seats and boomerangs.

*Looking for bargains*

The flea market, which packs up at 1pm, runs parallel to Trastevere to Porta Portese beside the **Sublicio** bridge opposite Capolinea, a tiny bus terminal (buses 56 and 60).

The section of Trastevere between the Viale and the river (apart from the flea market) tends to be smarter than the rest of Trastevere and contains several good restaurants.

If you can spare the time before eating to see a little-known work by the magnificent Gianlorenzo Bernini, head up the main street from the Porta Portese towards Viale Tastevere and make a short diversion to your right into the **Piazza San Francesco d'Assisi** to visit the church of the same name. There are some interesting paintings here, but in the Albertini chapel, immediately left of the altar, is a glorious reclining figure, *The Blessed Ludovica Albertoni*, her saintly face displaying a mystic ecstasy that is captivating. The lifelike hands, characteristic of Bernini, look as if they are made of silk rather than laboriously fashioned from marble. Another treasure to be admired in this little church is the work above the altar, *The Virgin and Child with St Anne*, by the Genovese artist known as Baciccio (1639–1709) who has been referred to as 'the Bernini of painting'.

Now along the Porto di Ripa Grande (*ripa* means 'riverside') to the far end of the sprawling ministry building (built in the 1790s as a poorhouse), turning inland for a short restaurant tour. First, in the pretty Piazza Mercanti, is the Da Meo Pattaca restaurant, then along Via Santa Cecilia is the India House restaurant, and in Via dei Vascellari you come to the Trattoria da Enzo. Turn left on Via dei Salumi past the Mameli school and up Vicolo del Buco to Gino and tiny Papa Re in the Piazza del Drago. At the right is Fidelio, a wine bar open until 2am.

*Palazzo Corsini*

Starting back at the Capolinea bus-stop (*capolinea* means 'head of the line'), dodge cars and motorcycles all the way along Via di San Francesco a Ripa past San Egidio to the central square of **Santa Maria in Trastevere.** Here you can sit at the Di Mirzio café and admire the 12th-century tower and fine mosaics of the church. Even at its busiest times the Piazza Santa Maria, with its 300-year-old fountain, is captivating. Children kick footballs and chase pigeons; tourists buy foreign papers and photograph each other; students hawk their poetry, and from the seats of stationary motorcycles cats eye passers-by warily.

In the adjoining little **Piazza San Egidio** is the **Folklore Museum** with a section devoted to the much-loved dialect poet of the last century Trilussa, whose lifesize statue stands beside the Acqua Paola fountain. The museum offers remarkably little to see for the admission charged.

Head out of the main square along Via della Scala to the splendid **Settimiano Arch**, named after a famous general and incorporated into the city walls in the 6th century. There's a nice little café beside the arch with outdoor tables from where you can watch the vibrant, ever-changing street scene. Off Via della Lungara, past the arch, then through a doorway and up an impressive stairway, is the 15th-century **Palazzo Corsini** which now houses the National Academy and Galleria Corsini (open till 2pm, closed Monday). The list of painters whose works are displayed includes Rubens, Caravaggio and Van Dyck.

In 1883, the palace gardens became the **Botanical Gardens** (closed at sunset), exceptionally charming with tinkling waterfalls, one of which runs between wide stairs leading to the upper level. There are thousands of different plant species, including a scented garden for the blind and a special collection of medicinal herbs. Across

*Gianicolo statues in Trastevere*

the street, the **Villa Farnesina** (Monday to Saturday 9am–1pm), built in 1508 by Baldassare Peruzzi for the Sienese banker Agostino Chigi, contains Raphael's classic *The Triumph of Galatea*. Much of the villa's gardens, which once stretched to the Tiber, were uprooted in the 19th-century when the river's embankments were constructed, but the interior of the villa is splendidly decorated, especially Peruzzi's **Sala della Prospettiva** with its clever *trompe l'oeil* frescoes. When the villa became the property of the Farnese family in 1580, there was an ambitious plan to link it to the Farnese palace across the Tiber but it came to naught.

The route along Lungara leads to the Vatican but we will go back through the Arch of Settimiano, and up the hill along **Via Garibaldi**, to visit the Gianicolo, the hill on which, in the 7th cen-

*Villa Farnesina*

tury BC, Tarquinius, the Etruscan leader, is said to have been standing when an eagle flew down to perch on his shoulder. He took it as a portent that he would rule Rome, which turned out to be the case.

From Garibaldi ascend the wide steps to the **Piazza San Pietro in Montorio**. In the precincts is Bernini's circular *Tempietto*. Continue beyond the Spanish Academy and up to the fabulous **Fontana Paola**. This fountain was erected in 1611 by Pope Paul, who restored Trajan's aqueduct bringing water from Lake Bracciano in the north. The No 41 bus (from G Carini) turns right here, past the ugly fascistera monument and busts of military heroes to the majestic statue of **Giuseppe Garibaldi** (1807–82), the hero who helped to unify Italy by conquering the south. There is a snack bar here and splendid views.

Heading back along Pancrazio, just before passing through the immense walls built by the 2nd-century emperor Aurelius, look for an old building bearing the name Michelangelo; today, sadly, it is merely a facade concealing water pipes. A little way down Via Giacomo Medici is the grandiose **American Academy**, which insists upon a letter of introduction before granting admission.

Keep left, heading downhill, to return to the main piazza. If you have time, however, you might enjoy a stroll in the largest and most peaceful park in Rome, the grounds of the **Villa Pamphili** behind the Gianicolo. (Walk from the arch along Via Aurelia Antica.) Pope Innocent X's nephew, Camillo Pamphili, laid out the lovely grounds and in 1652 built the villa, now a museum. The park contains many exotic trees including avocado pears and several varieties of palm, and a fountain originally designed for the Piazza Navona by Bernini now plays here in an orange grove.

*Piazza San Pietro – St Peter's Square*

DAY (4)

## The Vatican

**A morning in the Vatican museums, followed by St Peter's Square and the basilica**

*–Go early to the Vatican museums (they close at 1pm)–*

The relationship between the Vatican and the Italian state has occasionally been an uneasy one but in 1929 under the Lateran Treaty the Church was given the right to run its own affairs. The occasion was marked with the construction of the aptly-named **Via della Conciliazione**, a majestic tree-lined (and traffic-jammed) boulevard connecting St Peter's Square to the forbidding Castel Sant' Angelo which has been Vatican property for centuries.

The Vatican is a state within a state, with open borders which are well guarded after the gates close at 11pm. It has one of the largest libraries and the smallest number of automobiles in the world (about one in five of its residents has a car). It accredits ambassadors and legations from virtually every country in the world but has no room for them within its walls.

If you plan to head immediately to the

*The crux of Christianity*

museums from other parts of town, the easiest route is to take a taxi or bus No 49 (to Piazza del Risorgimento, then walk) or buses numbered 32, 51, 81 492, 907 or 991. The nearest underground station is Ottaviano on Line A.

Once there, you'll be amazed by how much can be packed into what, after all, is an area that covers less than half a square mile (40 hectares). It's worth buying the official *Guide to the Vatican Museums,* expensive as it is, although you can get a lot of pleasure by making your tour a random one, pausing to admire whatever catches your eye.

The 18th-century **spiral staircase** (by Giuseppe Momo) is a phenomena construction, as you'll realise if you stand at the top for a few moments and note that people coming up never meet those going down. Possibly the most famous work of antiquity in the Vatican is the marble **Laocoon** statue, in the **Pio-Clemente Museum**. A 1st-century copy by a trio of Rhodes sculptors of a bronze sculpture dating back to the 3rd-century BC, the statue was mentioned in the writings of Pliny the Elder (who died when Pompeii was wiped out by a volcanic eruption in AD79) but was lost until turning up again in 1506 when it was acquired by Pope Julius II.

The statue illustrates the tale told by Virgil in *The Aeneid* of the Trojan priest of Apollo who tried to warn his companions at Troy about the wooden horse in which the Greeks were about to infiltrate the city. Angered, the goddess Athene sent serpents to kill Laocoon. This

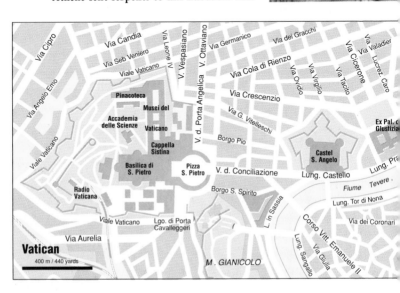

museum contains also a rich treasury of early Roman statuary, in particular the one entitled *Apoxyomenos* by the 3rd-century BC sculptor Lysippus (actually it's a 1st-century AD copy of the bronze original). Lysippus, who also made a statue of Alexander the Great, specialised in capturing the fleeting moment and here he movingly portrays the fatigue of an athlete after the big race has ended. The athlete is mopping his brow; the title is derived from the Greek word *apoxyein* ('to wipe off').

There's also a statue of Hermes, the messenger of the Olympian gods, which was found near Casteĺ Sant' Angelo, and a Roman copy in marble of a 4th-century BC Greek bronze, probably by Leochares, known as the *Apollo Belvedere* which once stood in the ancient agora in Athens. The renowned German archaeologist Johann Joachim Winckelmann said of it: 'of all the works of antiquity that have escaped destruction, the statue of Apollo represents the highest ideal of art.'

Before leaving the Pio-Clemente walk through the vestibule to see the wide staircase by Donato Bramante, who was also responsible for the courtyard itself. It was constructed at the request of Pope Julius II so that it could be ridden up on horseback.

For those with an interest in ancient civilisations, the **Etruscan Museum** is a must. Dominating the five or six centuries before the Roman kings arrived in the 8th century BC, the Etruscan civilisation was probably our last matriarchal society.

If you have only one morning for your visit to the Vatican museums, clearly you must make some choices. You can, if you wish, select from four colour-coded routes of which A is the shortest at about 90 minutes and D the most complete, but taking five hours.

The specific routes are as follows:

**A** (violet) classical art, sculptures, tapestries, charts, medieval fabrics, enamels and jewellery.

*In the Vatican*

***This way, please***

**B** (beige) adds Etruscan, Roman, early Christian and ethnological collections.

**C** (green) plus Egyptian, Roman, Raphael rooms, Fra Angelico frescoes, Borgia apartment with Pinturicchio works, modern sacred art, library.

**D** (yellow) takes in everything.

All include the **Sistine Chapel** which everybody wants to see. What the chapel is most renowned for, of course, are its frescoes by the great Michelangelo Buonarroti, although earlier works by Perugino, Pinturicchio, Boticelli and Piero di Cosimo were destroyed to make room for them. Commissioned by Sixtus's nephew, Pope Julius II, the artist began work in 1508 on the ceiling which was finally completed in 1512. Twenty-one years and three popes later, at the request of Pope Clement VII de' Medici, Michelangelo was recalled, this time to cover the altar wall with his *Last Judgement*. Containing 391 separate figures, this immense work (200 sq m/239 sq yds) took another three years. *The Guide to the Vatican Museums* carries detailed explanations but it is not necessary to read them to appreciate the beauty of the frescoes. Try viewing from different places, particularly from just inside the smaller room.

Not everybody was happy with the paintings. After one of the pope's aides, Biagio de Cesena, observed that the figures were 'more suitable for an inn', Michelangelo promptly placed the Monsignor along with Charon in the underworld, over which (the pope told him drily) he had no jurisdiction.

***'The Creation'***

Leading from the Sistine Chapel is a corridor lined with eye-catching old Latin and Greek gravestones ('To the very sweet pupil of mine, Aphelia', reads one) and then more statues: the 1st-century poet Sallustis, a doctor holding a caduceus and numerous two-headed busts of Janus, the ancient Roman deity who guarded gateways.

The spacious, formal couryard with its centrepiece, the golden *Sphera con Sphera* by modern sculptor Arnado Pomadoro (1990), and a colossal head of Augustus offers a welcome break before you enter the **Pinacoteca** with its wealth of religious art spanning the 11th to 19th century. Some of the bigger frescoes were 'the cartoons of their time', biblical scenes of stories installed in small, rural churches to educate the peasants.

In particular note the (badly-lit) Leonardo da Vinci portrait of *St Jerome* in room X; Guido Rini's *The Crucifixion of St Peter* – all light and emotion – in room XIII; and the most famous picture in the collection, *Deposition* by Caravaggio (who is said by some to have 'invented light'), also reproduced in the lobby.

A bus runs from the museums to St Peter's but you can also get there by walking along **Viale Vaticano** beside the towering walls.

The museum bus allows you to see some of the grounds, including the **Chinese Pavilion**, the **Papal Academy of Science** and the **Eagle Fountain** where the water from the Acqua Paola acqueduct first reached the Vatican. You'll also pass the remains of the wall built by Pope Leo IV in the 9th century; the Vatican radio station (FM105 for regular news in many languages) has its headquarters here.

*Painting by Raphael*

Among the things you will not see are the pope's rarely-used private railway, the heliport, the supermarket and the printing works, from which emerges the daily newspaper *L'Osservatore Romano* and Catholic literature in a vast range of languages.

**St Peter's Basilica** and the immense circular piazza over which it presides are intended to awe and certainly manage to do so. Early in the 15th century Donato Bramante, at the invitation of Pope Julius II, was the first of a string of architects who began planning the new church, but it was almost a century and a half before building was completed.

Michelangelo designed the magnificent dome, which, after his death in 1514, was finished according to his plans. The enormous **piazza**, designed in the 1650s by the great Gianlorenzo Bernini, is semi-enclosed by 284 gigantic columns in four rows, the passage between them so arranged that viewed from a central spot the colon-

nades appear to be a solitary row. A perfect fusion of art and mathematics.

An Egyptian **obelisk**, said to have taken the energies of 900 men to raise, is now the piazza's central feature and is surrounded by whimsically-patterned tiles depicting the winds. It once stood on the spot where Christians were martyred and later in Nero's circus.

Bernini carved the statue on the left and his pupils were responsible for the 140 statues on the balustrade plus the 13 others crowning the basilica itself. The facade was by Carlo Maderna who also designed one of the fountains.

The pope makes an appearance at one of the fourth floor windows of his living quarters (on the right) every Sunday at noon and blesses the faithful in St Peter's at 11am on Wednesday mornings in winter, in the vast piazza on Wednesday afternoons during the rest of the year.

The basilica's interior is breathtaking, a huge area culminating in Bernini's immense *baldacchino* (canopy) in front of the altar, above which a dove glows from the natural light through a golden window. Overhead is the enormous 119-m (390-ft) high **dome** designed by Michelangelo and Bramante which can be reached via stairs or a lift (open until 4.45pm in winter, 6.15pm in summer; admission charge). Bernini's elaborate monument to Pope Urban VIII is by the altar and his last work, a monument to Pope Alexander VII, completed in 1678, is on the left. He was also responsible for the statue of Constantine the Great in the portico. The statue of Charlemagne, on the right, was sculpted by Cornacchini some 65 years later.

The single most important artwork in the church is Michelangelo's exquisite *La Pietà*, just right of the entrance. The signature on the Virgin's sash is the only one on any of Michelangelo's works and is said to have been surreptitiously carved by the artist after the statue's installation when word reached him that it was being attributed to someone else. Since the attack by a hammer-wielding maniac in 1972, *La Pietà* has been protected by bullet-proof glass.

*La Pietà*

Almost always full of people, the spacious basilica (the aisles at each side are 76m/250ft in length) never seems crowded unless a Mass is taking place. Occasionally, the throngs part to allow the passage of a platoon of the Swiss Guards in their distinctive orange-trimmed blue uniforms.

The subterranean **grottoes** (entrance near the statue of St Peter by the canopy) contain the tombs of early popes including one believed to be that of St Peter.

*St Peter and the key to heaven*

# PICK & MIX

## 1. The Spine of Rome

**Along the Via del Corso, from Piazza del Popolo to Piazza Colonna.**
*See map on pages 18–19.*

The spine of Rome is the broad boulevard called the **Via del Corso**,
running from Piazza del Popolo to Piazza Venezia. It's a metaphor
of Italian life, of Roman life. Pedestrians invade it and make it
into the biggest and most renowned *struscio* (in Spanish, *paseo*).

In other words, it's a promenading, parading, win-
dow-watching but mostly people-watching street.
The young go to eye each other with romance on
their minds; the old to watch for signs of power
and the decline of mores.

**Piazza del Popolo** has two lovely churches,
one on each side of the Corso, and two famous,
smart cafés. On the left, **Canova** is the café
where the more conventional types go. It offers class, good service, understated style. On
the other side is **Rosati**, the just-as-elegant
but slightly transgressive bar where the Italian *Dolce Vita* took place. Here was the meeting place, the pick-up place, the place where
real and fake movie directors, real and fake
producers, real and fake actors and actresses,
real and fake starlets would gather in the
late afternoon, before moving to Via
Veneto for the rest of the evening and night.

Via Veneto is dead now. What's left are big hotels, big empty
bars and two newsvendors who stay open late. Rosati isn't exactly
dead, it still retains an aura of the glory days. You can still eat at
the **Bolognese** next door and feel you're in the midst of things.

You'll certainly be in the midst of art if you go to the Renaissance church of **Santa Maria del Popolo**, on where you can see a glorious *Birth of Christ* by Pinturicchio, two great dramatic Caravaggios,
the Cappella Chigi designed by Raphael, a Del Piombo's *Birth of
Mary* over the altar, a Lorenzetti *Jonah and the Whale* sketched by
Raphael and two sculptures by Bernini. Also here is the tomb of Pope

*Piazza del Popolo*

Alexander VI (Cardinal Borgia), lover of Vanezza Caltanei who bore him four children.

Alexander VI, who was elected to the papacy in the year in which Columbus discovered America (1492) was the pope so hated by Martin Luther, who journeyed down to Rome determined to fight what he saw as the degeneration and debauchery of the Church. When he arrived on a cold December day in 1510 he stayed at the Augustinian convent attached to Santa Maria and held Mass there. After that Bernini, at the pope's suggestion, removed the altar, and according to rumour Luther's cell was turned into a toilet.

The three main streets leading from the Piazza del Popolo are known as the *tridente*. The central one is the Corso. With your back to the Aurelian walls at the piazza's northern end, go down **Via di Ripetta**, which is the one on the right. Soon you'll see some graffiti, the work of students from the Roman Academy of Painting, who make the area so lively. Next is a quiet, rather mournful-looking grave mound with the urns of several emperors – Augustus, Tiberius, Claudius and Nerva – circled by cypresses. Nearby, on the other side of the road, is a strange, ugly, squat building encased in glass, the **Ara Pacis** (Tuesday to Saturday 9am–1.30pm). This is the altar to the Augustan peace that began in 13BC and continued for several decades after the emperor's death in AD14, giving to the Roman Empire, and indeed the world, the only century without major wars to date.

After this rather strange encounter, re-

*Ara Pacis*

*Befriending a local inhabitant*

turn to the Corso and soon, on your right after the fashionable Via dei Condotti, you'll come to the **Piazza Colonna**, notable for its 30-m (100-ft) high column of Marcus Aurelius, an early fan of Greek culture whose 19-year reign endeared him to his subjects. The column, decorated with reliefs of the emperor's foreign campaigns, is now topped with a statue of St Paul and 5m (15ft) of its base are buried underground.

Famous palaces flank the square. The **Palazzo Chigi**, built by a Sienese banker; and the **Palazzo Wedekind** adorned by 16 magnificent pillars. Adjoining the Piazza Colonna with its Galleria Colonna, the only big glass-covered gallery in Rome, is the **Piazza Montecitorio**, well-known to all Italians because it is where the *Parlamento* is housed in the Palazzo Monetecitorio

Here also, opposite each other on the Corso, are the two big temples to mass Italian fashion: La Rinascente for adult customers (four floors) and Babilonia for the youth (just a single, hectic ground floor). The feeling among Romans is that apart from these two establishments all the other clothes shops overflowing from the Corso windows make the street a bit tacky. There's talk about saving the Corso from too much commercialisation, and of restoring the best and more elegant 19th-century buildings. Until then, however, it's just a *struscio* for young suburbanites. Elegance is confined to the three streets that lead off the Corso to Piazza di Spagna, but the two worlds, however close, hardly ever mix.

## 2. Popes and Heretics

**A half-day tour visiting the Castel Sant' Angelo, Piazza Farnese and Campo dei Fiori.** *See map pages 18–19.*

Hadrian, the emperor-philosopher, designed and built his own mausoleum beside the Tiber in the year 139AD in what is now central Rome. Today it is the **Castel Sant' Angelo** (Monday to Friday 9am–1.30pm).

The mausoleum was the beginning of a construction that became part of emperor Aurelian's walls, then a fortified citadel, a stronghold of Rome's defences during the lone, dark ages when Rome was at the mercy of northern invaders and marauders in search of the city's riches, fabled marbles and gold. It was Pope Gregory the Great who named the citadel Castel Sant' Angelo in 590AD after a vision of an angel heralded the end of a plague in the city.

In 1277, a wall and passageway were built linking the castle to the already huge Vatican palaces. It's still here to be seen one block away from the Via della Conciliazione and you should visit it, starting from the castle itself and going to the Vatican. It was also a defence from which to keep the strategic *borgo* area under control.

Arrows and missiles were thrown from its bastion when King Charles VIII of France invaded Rome in 1494. Alexander VI, the Borgia pope, lived with hundreds of people in the besieged castle but it was not captured. The castle was attacked again in 1527 when Pope Clement VII took refuge there while the troops, commanded by the Constable of Bourbon, ransacked Rome. The pope saw the flames of the city from his refuge and could do nothing about it. The castle held out, however, and saved his life.

The best approach is from its own bridge, **Ponte Sant' Angelo**, the most spectacular of all the city's bridges over the Tiber. Hadrian built it when he made his mausoleum and it lasted 15 centuries until collapsing in 1450 under the strain of a holy year that brought masses of pilgrims to the city. It was duly rebuilt, incorporating the ruins and in the 17th century Bernini and his pupils sculpted the figures of angels that grace it. The gigantic Archangel Michael with his sword at the ready is a later work by a Flemish sculptor, the 18th-century Pieter Wershaffelt.

Inside the graceful but imposing Castel Sant'Angelo are artefacts from all periods of Roman history, from the Chamber of the Urns, where the ashes of Hadrian's family lie (Hadrian himself ended up buried in his beloved villa at Tivoli, in the hills south of Rome) to the 58 stately rooms that made up the pope's palace. It certainly has no lack of pomp, frescoes or art, nor of creature comforts (you can even still see a pope's private lavatory) in this typical Renaissance palace.

Castel Sant' Angelo makes a perfect visit if you have children or teenagers with you: they'll be captivated by the dungeons, the cannons and piles of cannon balls, and the small but fascinating museum of arms. Not the least of its attractions is the café with its splendid view of Rome, a rare feature in a city that often considers its monuments too serious to be made comfortable.

*Castel Sant' Angelo*

**Via Giulia**, the 16th-century street built by Donato Bramante for Pope Julius II, is lined with *palazzi*, churches and antique shops, beginning with the Florentine-style church of **San Giovanni dei Fiorentini** (containing the tomb of Borromini, who designed the altar). It was the first main street of Renaissance Rome and to make it the builders sliced through a jumble of narrow medieval streets, some of which run off Via Giulia itself. In July the street is lit by hundreds of oil lamps and the courtyards and cloisters are open to classical concerts. The setting is so exquisite and romantic that even non-music lovers should try to visit at this time. (Check exact dates beforehand, as they change from year to year.)

At the lower end of the street a lovely archway spans the road. It's one of Michelangelo's projects that was never completed because of lack of funds. He originally planned to link Palazzo Farnese and its gardens with the Villa Farnesina on the other side of the Tiber (an extravagant concept that says a lot about Michelangelo and even more about such Renaissance princes as Farnese, Borgia, Borghese and their families). Instead, we're left with this rather romantic, ivy-covered archway and the curious **Fontana del Mascherone**. It's an ancient, Roman mask, to which a granite basin was added, and which was fused with the baroque fountain on the right, a rare example of two period pieces being combined to produce a third. Near the arch is the **Palazzo Falconieri** and, with its faded fresco facade, the **Palazzo Ricci**.

Turn left off Via Giulia and you'll arrive in the enchanting **Piazza Farnese**, with its two fountains, the Palazzo Farnese, and church, linked by a short street to the other unique square, Campo dei Fiori. In Piazza Farnese, large enough for the sun to fill it all day, examine the two magnificent fountains whose basins were stolen from the Caracalla Baths.

The **Palazzo Farnese**, in which Michelangelo's genius played a not inconsiderable part – the biggest front window is his – is the pro-

*Rome's ochre-coloured rooftops*

totype of all the other Renaissance palaces. It was conceived as a magnificent, even bigger structure but was scaled down when the young Sangallo finished it. From the square you can see only the facade of the palace which has an internal courtyard, frescoed salons, and a galleria painted by Annibale Carracci. It was given to the French State for a symbolic 100 lire for services rendered to the pope in the 19th century. You can view the inside on Sundays, between 10am and noon.

Now to **Campo dei Fiori**, called the field of flowers because at the very beginning it *was* a field of flowers. The fruit, vegetables and fish market has been here from the start, and it was always one of Rome's liveliest squares where cardinals, fishmongers, pilgrims, vegetable sellers and ladies of disrepute would rub shoulders. This is probably the only square without a church.

In ancient times, the piazza was surrounded by inns for pilgrims, travellers and later, from the 17th century onwards, visitors to Rome. There are still hotels here and if you are romantically inclined, you might like to stay in one. In the 15th century, some were owned by successful courtesans, the most famous of whom was Vannozza Catanei, mistress of Pope Alexander VI Borgia. On the corner of the square and Via del Pellegrino, you can see her shield which she had decorated with her own coat of arms and those of her husband and lover, the Borgia pope.

With its reputation for being a carnal, pagan place, it seemed a natural spot to hold executions. Giordano Bruno was the most important figure to die at the stake, burned alive in the middle of the square. A philosopher and priest, he was tagged a heretic and found guilty of free-thinking. He preached a more harmonious concept of God and the universe, saying that Earth was not the centre of it, but was revolving around the sun. The ecclesiastical authorities tried hard to make him repent, but when they were certain he wouldn't they burned him on a chilly morning in February, 1600. Now you can inspect the imposing statue of him, hooded and sombre, with a book in his hands. Today, surrounded by young people and vagrants, travellers and pilgrims of a new kind, Giordano Bruno still keeps his own people under his wing.

The square also has a couple of smart cafés, a good restaurant, a cinema (with English films sometimes on Mondays) and a good Chinese restaurant (at the beginning of Via dei Giubbonari), and a chic, popular wine bar.

## 3. A Museum Trip through History

**There are 150 museums in Rome altogether. Here is a tour taking in a few of them, from the Etruscans through Roman times to the 18th century.**

If you want to immerse yourself fully in ancient Rome, the museums where you can feel it, smell it, touch it, see it are your best bet. All you'll need are a bit of patience, imagination, and this chapter. It will have to be a fast ride through many centuries, from

before the austere and somewhat grim birth of Rome, as an outlaws' village, to the splendour of the Augustan times, when Roman emperors ruled over the entire pacified world while Christianity grew inside it, to the slow crumbling of the colossal structure that left the door open to barbarian invasions.

Our story begins with the Etruscans, a civilised, peace-loving, fascinating people whose women lived as

*Etruscan sculpture in the Villa Giulia*

freely as the men. They were ruled by sorcerer kings, men who according to legend could order lightning, predict the future and change the course of lives. Great builders with a splendid agriculture, they believed so strongly in the afterlife that they left us with necropolises that are bigger than their actual towns, which numbered 12. They ruled in Tuscany and Latium for almost a millennium. We know surprisingly little about them. We don't know where they came from, nor can we understand their

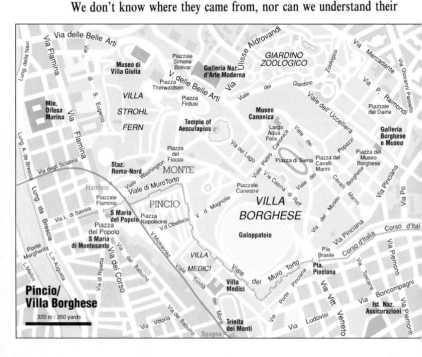

*Museo Nazionale Romano's cloisters*

language. It's a mystery to historians why they let the Roman up-starts take over, when they could have smashed them and prevailed for at least a century more. At the time Rome was just an outlaws' village. The first three Roman kings were Etruscans, a fact not widely known, and the Roman empire's masons, gods, agriculture, sewage, roads, administration and system of government – all that we know as Roman, and great – is an Etruscan heritage. When Rome became strong, its major priority was apparently to destroy the Etruscan towns. Only two bronze statues out of the thousands that decorated Etruscan cities are left, but some bronze works are on show in the **Museo di Villa Giulia** at one corner of the elegant Borghese gardens. So it is here, in what was the villa of Pope Julius III, the last great pope of the Renaissance, that we begin our tour through Rome's history.

The Etruscans worked wonders with metal from the bronze that they exported to Greece (classical Greece imported tripods for 15 altars from Etruria) and to the rest of the Mediterranean people, including the Egyptians. They made wonderful jewellery – their filigree and granular technique was so subtle and sophisticated that only Benvenuto Cellini, the Renaissance master, was able to recreate it perfectly. Sadly, the museum is badly presented, but the masterpieces at least speak for themselves. Especially enticing are the *Apollo of Veyo* with his ineffable smile, the intriguing ancestor of the Gioconda's smile; and *The Couple* where

*Statue of Juno*

dignity, tranquillity and vision in both the man and the woman imply a civilisation unrivalled for depth of emotional feelings.

The villa itself was a country retreat more than a permanent house or *palazzo,* with gardens and pavilions designed by Vignola. Enjoy the quiet beauty of a 16th-century garden while looking at a reconstruction of an Etruscan temple made by Count Adolfo Cozza, copying the temple of Alatri.

We move forward in history to Roman times with a visit to the imposing Palazzo Massimo, containing the **Museo Nazionale**

**Romano**, to the left of the Piazzale dei Cinquecento as you leave the railway station. Here you'll have the best introduction to the Roman world, with many original statues and copies of Greek statues and a wealth of Roman artefacts on show.

Follow this with a visit to the **Piazza del Campidoglio**, designed by Michelangelo and considered to be the heart of Rome past and present. Climb the imposing steps leading to the square to reach the **Musei Capitolini** which occupy two different buildings (but just one ticket; free for under 16s and over 60s with proof). Start with the building on the left: on entering the courtyard you'll be confronted by a gigantic, reclining sea god and the statue of Marcus Aurelius on his horse, the single most imposing piece of all the ancient Roman statuary left to us. As you go upstairs you'll see several masterpieces of the golden period of Roman rule. You can feel a powerful sense of both the strength and the calm of a society that conquered the world.

If it's a good day you'll be able to go to the balcony and look down at the square from above. It's in the form of a trapezium, with classical statues of relevance to Rome and Renaissance buildings designed by Michelangelo. The square faces west, towards St Peter's. Michelangelo had a clear understanding of the two great forces of Rome, the Roman empire, symbolised by this Capitol, and the Vatican, where the spiritual power had its earthly seat.

While passing through the piazza and courtyard en route to the second of the Capitolini museums, you will notice the colossal head of the emperor Constantine, a 4th-century piece depicting the larger-than-life attitude that would eventually bring his downfall. The hand and other fragments of the statue are just as impressive.

It is in the adjoining **Palazzo dei Conservatori** (*see Day 2, page 25*) that the transition from the Romans to the Renaissance will gracefully unfold before your eyes. The fare on display is almost too rich, but you should remember that this big building was the seat

*'The Dying Gaul', one of the Musei Capitolini's finest exhibits*

*Capitoline statue*

of the city's magistrates since the late Middle Ages (hence the frescoes) and remains an official building to this day. It has collected almost as many works of art for display as the Vatican.

Here is the single bronze piece, *The She-wolf*, that links the Etruscans and the Romans. It also links the Romans to the Renaissance, because the two twins were added by a Renaissance sculptor around the 15th century.

Now we'll continue our race through history with a 10-minute walk (unfortunately through busy 20th-century traffic) away from the Forum and into the Piazza Venezia. From the foot of the steps you can gaze up at the balcony from which Mussolini used to address the crowds.

Turn left into Corso Vittorio Emanuele II to visit the **Museo Barracco** (9am–1pm), at No 168. It's a compact museum with Egyptian, Greek and Roman sculptures. In this small exhibition, which is the founder's personal collection, it's possible to trace the links between the three civilisations. Next, go along Vittorio Emanuele for 550m (600yds) to Campo dei Fiori, the lovely square cheek by jowl with Piazza Farnese, north of the Ponte Sisto. Just behind Campo dei Fiori is the Piazza Capo di Ferro where you'll find the **Galleria Spada** (9am–2pm). Here is displayed  some of the best art of the 17th century: Rubens (1577–1640) and Caravaggio (1571–1610), Guido Reni (1575–1642) and Guercino (1591–1666), Domenichino (1581–1641) and Brueghel the Elder (c1525–69). But these works are just the *hors d'oeuvre* to those in the two other magnificent museums.

First is the **Galleria Nazionale d'Arte Antica** (9am–1pm), at Palazzo Barberini, Via delle Quattro Fontane 13, a great *palazzo* built by Bernini for one of the greatest families. It houses masterpieces from the 13th to the 16th century and it will add at a future date 17th- and 18th-century paintings from the Palazzo Corsini, another *palazzo* full of pieces collected through the centuries. It will then be a gallery of paintings tracking the important centuries following the dark Middle Ages, when Rome was reduced to the state of a small village among the ruins of a glorious past. For century after century during this period, it was harassed by invaders. The Castel Sant' Angelo is, among other things, a formidable reminder of the battles of Rome (and its popes who were then its rulers).

*Caravaggio's 'Bacchino Malato'*

Our final segment, in this time-trip, is a visit to another private collection of a great family. This is in the **Villa Borghese** which the state bought from the family. Major renovation and restructuring are continuing here, so you may be limited to only the ground floor, but it's still worthwhile if only to see *Apollo and Daphne* by a young Bernini – the genius whose prodigious works can be encountered all over Rome, starting from the big fountain at Piazza Navona – and the very famous statue of Pauline Borghese, by the classical sculptor Canova. Canova tried to recapture the beauty and strength of the classical statues and managed to add something of his own vision with a polished, almost cold sensuality that reflects his personal style. If the museum's 19th-century and modern art section is open, you'll be able to admire Canova's 18th-century work, this being the most 'modern' so far on our journey through Roman art history.

If you want to pursue your search there are innumerable smaller museums to visit, some of them little jewels. A complete listing of museums, their schedules and their contents can be found in a booklet called *Qui Roma* ('Here's Rome') available free in various languages at the EPT (*Ente Provinciale del Turismo*), Via Parigi 5, near the Termini station, just off the big Piazza Esedra. Incidentally, this square boasts a big fountain built in the last century by the grandfather of the mayor, Rutelli.

*Masterpiece in marble*

**From the Caracalla Baths to the Via Appia and the Catacombs.
Morning tour.**

*–Take No 18 bus along the Appian Way–*

'Here I am a man, here I can be a man,' said the ancient Romans
when they went to the baths, the meeting-place for everyone from
the emperor downwards. Going to the communal
baths was a way of life for the Roman upper
classes, which included the senators and the
wealthy, but there were baths for the ordinary
citizens and soldiers too. In fact, wherever the
Romans conquered, they built baths which, along
with their roads and water and sewage systems,
became the mark of their civilisation. Reflect-
ing the times in which they were built, they
were simple and sensible during the republican
era and sophisticated, complex and luxurious
in the days of the emperors, becoming decadent towards the end of their rule.

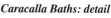

The most popular to visit today are the **Baths
of Caracalla** (open weekdays until 6pm in summer, 3pm in winter) which are almost on the edge

*Caracalla Baths: detail*

of the city and enclosed by the Aurelian walls. Emperor Caracalla
opened them in AD217, after which they functioned for 300 years until destroyed by the invading Goths. What remains is still impos-

ing enough to demonstrate
bathing procedures (1,500
people could bathe at
once). At the entrance is
the work-out room and
then the gymnasium with
its lovely patterned mo-
saic floors.

Just as today one would
experience rooms with different temperatures so
there was the tepidarium
(fairly warm), the frigi-
darium (cold, as you
might guess) and a sauna.

As going to baths was
not just about bathing,
there were also Latin and
Greek libraries, a lecture
room and a chapel dedica-
ted to Mithra, a blood-
thirsty god favoured by

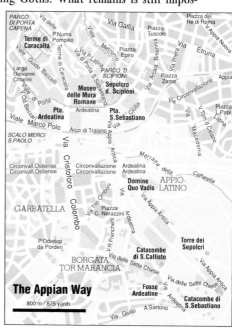

**The Appian Way**

800 m / 875 yards

*Tombs of Scipioni*

the army whose legionnaires carried his worship to the furthest points of the empire. There was also a place for swimming, an open-air stadium and a massage room.

The Caracalla Baths were richly decorated with beautiful mosaics but few are left today, because the Farnese family plundered them in the 15th century to decorate their palace near Campo dei Fiori. Today the French embassy is housed here and the rest of the mosaics are still preserved. In July and August operas are staged at the baths.

From the Caracalla Baths it's a short walk to the **Tombs of the Scipioni**. The Scipioni were a family of generals, one of whom, Scipio Africanus, as he came to be known, defeated Hannibal at the beginning of the 3rd century BC. The Columbarium houses the urns containing their ashes.

The street on which they are located is called **Via di Porta San Sebastiano**, which takes its name from a famous gate in the old walls built by Aurelian (161–80) to defend Rome from marauding German tribes.

As in other parts of the city, the walls are immense (12m/40ft high and 3½m/12ft thick) and at one time they stretched for 18km (11 miles) with 381 towers and 18 gates of which **San Sebastiano** was one. (It was originally called Porta Appia but the Christians renamed it after the basilica and catacombs of the saint nearby.) When the Christians beat the Muslim fleet at Lepanto in 1571, their chief, Marcantonio Colonna, led a triumphal procession from the Appian Way to this gate, the last Rome had. Now the towers house a museum (9am–1.30pm, closed Monday) with prints and models illustrating the history of the walls. This is one of the few places where you can actually walk along the walls and see how everything was incorporated into them – for example, Cestius's pyramid, the Porta Maggiore arches of the aqueduct southeast of the Termini station, and Hadrian's mausoleum.

The famous **Appian Way** begins here, although if you want to see it vaguely resembling the way it used to be, you'll have to take No 118 bus to the end of the line and begin your walk there. In parts it's still shaded with cypresses and pine trees, and paved with some of the original polygonal cobblestones (*basoli*).

Considering the date it was built – 312BC by Appius Claudius, a city official – the road is a remarkable piece of engineering. Its builders conquered marshes, kept it straight for the first 90km (56 miles) and linked part of it to a parallel canal which allowed travellers to alternate the carriage or horseback trip with a boat ride. The standard width (4.2m/14ft) allowed two carriages to pass with a pedestrian way at each side. Every 10–17km (7–12 miles) there were resting places, where travellers could change horses or stay overnight. Where the highway passed towns it was flanked by great villas and sometimes tombs or other monuments.

Frequently lengthened over the centuries, the Appian Way eventually went as far as Brindisi, the port on Italy's southeast coast which is almost 640km (400 miles) from Rome.

Wealthy families not only liked living along the road but many of them also chose to be buried along it, which is why there are so many tombs. These begin outside the city walls (it was forbidden to bury people within the city itself), notably with the gloomy **Catacombs of San Sebastiano**. Room after room, passageway after passageway has been cut into that soft, volcanic, porous stone called *tufo*, containing thousands of niches called *locule*, each with

*Outside the Catacombs of St Calixtus*

two or three bodies. Probably there are 100,000 people buried here altogether. The part that you can visit includes the Crypt of the Popes, where the early popes were buried, and that of St Cecilia.

Don't be confused by any references to the **Catacombs of San Calixtus** because they are joined underground to those of San Sebastiano, the entire complex taking up four levels altogether (only one may be visited) and stretching for 400m (4,400ft) underground. The San Sebastiano tombs were the first to be called catacombs after the Greek *Kata Kymbas* meaning 'near the caves'.

After passing the **Basilica of San Sebastiano**, which is almost opposite the mausoleum of Romulus (son of the 4th-century AD emperor of that name) in its own little park, you will notice ahead of you a cylindrical tower on the hill on the left. This is the **Tomb of Cecilia Metella**, built around 50BC, for the daughter of Quintus Metellus Creticus (conqueror of Crete). She later married Crassus whose father was one of the triumvirate that ruled Rome from 60–50BC (the other two being Caesar and Pompey).

The fortress-like tomb, decorated with sculptured marble, was put to good use in the 14th century by the upstart Caetari family, relatives of Giotto's patron Pope Boniface VIII, who used to exact tolls from passers-by. Lord Byron wrote about Cecilia Metella in his poem *Childe Harold,* but few facts of her life are known.

Over to the left of the tomb is the immense **Circus Maximus** – 520m (5,700ft) long, 52m (170ft) wide – where chariot racing was watched by crowds of more than 10,000 spectators. It is flanked by the ruins of an imperial palace.

Once past the **Via Cecilia Metella**, 5km (3 miles) from the city, the more attractive portion of the Via Appia begins. From here, in gentle countryside, the tombs come thick and fast. A free leaflet/map identifying them, *La Via Antica Appia,* is available from the office of EPT (Ente Provinciale del Turismo) at Via Parigi 11, near Termini station.

*Cecilia commemorated*

IN MEMORY OF EDITH CECIL... ...PIER OF NEW YORK U.S.A.

S. CAECILIA

## 5. The Jewish Quarter and Tiber Island

**Piazza Mattei, Portico d'Ottavia and Tiber Island, which is associated with healing.**

We begin our tour at the **Piazza Mattei**, a lovely small square with the most elegant, delicate and exquisite of fountains which, given the beauty of Roman fountains in general, is high praise. It is called *Fontana delle Tartarughe* (Tortoise fountain) and was made by Matteo Landini in 1584. It depicts four graceful, slender boys holding a dolphin on one hand and trying to push a tortoise into the upper basin with the other. Get close to those lovely hands and see if you would have realised that the tortoises were added later, by another sculptor.

*Kosher butcher at Portico*

Opposite the fountain is Palazzo Mattei, now housing a music academy called the Emerotica which sells records. It's a public building, so you can go to the top and enjoy a view of the Jewish quarter.

At the centre of this area is the **Portico d'Ottavia**. To reach it, turn into Piazza Lovatelli and proceed along Via Sant' Angelo in Peschia. The Portico is what's left of a hall of columns, 118m (388ft) wide by 135m (450ft) deep, which was erected in 147BC by Metellus, its function being a place to display the statues captured from Greece by the Roman armies. In some ways this was the very first Roman museum; Augustus, the emperor, dedicated it to his sister Octavia, the abandoned wife of Mark Antony, hence the name.

Gregorovius, the chronicler, noted: 'It was here that Vespasianus and Titus led the procession of victory over Israel with ceremonial displays.' It had been a very bitter war, and it was a very bitter, definitive defeat for the Jews, who scattered across the empire. Some went to live across the river in Trastevere, and others settled in this neighbourhood.

Some of the Jews already here had been brought to Rome as slaves by Pompey, and had come to be appreciated for their financial and medical skills. But when Christianity took over the Empire, Jews were branded 'murderers of God' and heretics. In the Middle Ages, by contrast, they enjoyed relative freedom and prosperity. One of the anti-popes, Anacletus, came from a converted Jewish family.

It was Pope Paul IV Caraffa who, on 26 July 1556, ordered the Jews to be forcibly moved to the area around the Portico d'Ottavia and what was from then on called the ghetto, or 'Jew-pit'. They

were permitted to leave the ghetto only if they were wearing a yellow hat if male, or a yellow veil if female, even during daylight hours. Jewish doctors were forbidden to treat Christian patients and generally banned from trading with Christians. Some left, some stayed. Those who stayed were confined to this ghetto, surrounded by high walls, with doors locked from the outside at night. On Sundays they were made to go to the nearby church of Sant' Angelo in Pescheria and forced to listen to Christian sermons. This continued until 1848.

The unification of Italy improved matters but then, when World War II started, persecution began again. The fascist regime shipped the Jews off to German concentration camps, although many well-meaning Italians deplored this and helped in any way they could.

There are still many Jews living around here. There are now dozens of kosher shops and a big synagogue which was built in 1874 when the new Italian state was conducting fierce political battles with the papacy, reducing its possessions to what is the Vatican City today. The Italian state finally made peace with the Church in the 1920s. In fact it was Mussolini, the fascist dictator, who settled the account. The relationship between the pope and the Jewish community is now good and constantly improving.

The Jewish quarter, walled or not, was always too cramped for the people who lived there, and was also too marshy to be very healthy. But it had a small but very active port facing the Tiber Island – the strangely beautiful island that the Romans connected with the mainland from the beginning, first with a wooden bridge and then a stone one.

Legend has it that in 293BC a plague forced the Romans to ask the Greeks for help, the Greek god Asclepius in particular. They were sent a ship full of snakes (it was with their venom that Asclepius, doctors cured major ills, with dream therapy also playing a part). The plague was stamped out, and the island was dedicated to curing the sick.

The church of **San Bartolomeo** in the beautiful central square of the island was built on the ruins of the temple of Asclepius (Aesculapius to the Romans) in the 10th century. The **Ponte Fabricio**, a footbridge connecting the ghetto to the island, was built in 62BC and is still in use, although unfortunately cars are also allowed on it today. The other bridge, **Ponte Cestio**, connecting the island to the Trastevere side, is inscribed with the names of the Byzantine emperors who restored it in AD370, when they were strong enough to have authority over Rome. The big medieval tower belonged to the powerful families who used to control the river and the area: first the Pierleonis family, then the Caetanis.

The big building with cars parked in front of it is the hospital. It has been there, in different shapes and sizes since that 3rd-century plague. The island is said to be in the shape of a ship if you look at it from middle distance, and it still has the sign of the caduceus, the two snakes wrapped around the stick, that is the symbol of Aesculapius tucked away somewhere at the downriver end. See if you can find it among the lovers who stroll the Tiber's banks on sunny days.

## 6. Arts and Crafts

**From mosaics to classy windows, from pocket sundials to 'Ancient Roman' jewellery. Afternoon tour, in the area south of Piazza di Spagna.**

Is a Roman statue a work of art and a splendid knob to a Renaissance *portone*, or a Cellini piece, just craft? Where's the dividing line? This question continually pops up when you are walking the quieter streets in the heart of Rome. When you chance upon a fountain, so delicate, so enchanting (the Fontana delle Tartarughe for example, in Piazza Mattei, the heart of the Jewish quarter) you ask yourself: is a fountain a work of art, or a practical piece of craft? It is no idle question in Rome. Art here has always been the celebration of power, from the Titus Arch that dominates part of the Forum to the Bernini canopy under Michelangelo's dome in St Peter's. Celebration, pomp, a will to state your strength and your values, as the Romans did, a will to state the reasons of religion, and its form of immortality.

But a fountain? A pipeline? A tool, an iron grate, a balcony,

*Fontana delle Tartarughe*

a toga, an exquisite Biagiotti cashmere sweater, an Armani jacket?

Art and craft are sisters (brothers?) of the same blood. There's a continuity, from doorknobs to fountains to statues and buildings, all the way from ancient Roman through the Middle Ages, the Renaissance, the baroque era and to the present day.

In Piazza Farnese there is an elegant showroom called **Farnese** displaying tiles with motifs that begin in Roman times and reach into the contemporary, touching all the periods of the history of Roman (which often meant Western) art and craft. Another place where you can see this historical continuity and intermingling of art and craft lies along the **Via dei Cappellari**, a narrow, medieval

street overflowing with cupboards and cabinets, tables and beds, where you can see craftsmen working at their trade, restoring old pieces of furniture, sometimes remaking them just as they were.

Another road within walking distance from here, close to the Sant' Angelo bridge, is **Via dei Coronari**, where you can watch restora-

*Cabinet and painting*

tions of elegant old furniture in a hotchpotch of styles down to an art nouveau lamp. Prices in Cappellari are reasonable and at times even very cheap. Coronari is, however, not cheap and it can be dangerously expensive if you fall in love with a piece.

The same goes for **Largo Fontanella Borghese**, near which a dozen or more elegant stalls offer everything from prints of the inevitable Piranesi, or Roman scenery that everybody wants to take home, to some dubious but fascinating pieces, and also some real forgotten treasures.

Is gold art or craft? There is Cartier in Paris, Tiffany's in New York, Asprey's in London, and in Rome it's **Bulgari.** It's the most elegant place in **Via dei Condotti**. If you don't dare to go inside, where an awesome atmosphere reigns, you can always peer through the box-like windows which display an array of fabulous jewellery. Bulgari, of course, offers Renaissance pieces too, which puts him ahead of rivals in Paris, London and New York.

In the smart trio of streets leading off the Piazza di Spagna you will find Valentino, Armani, Versace, Laura Biagiotti and Di Donato – another form of art and craft. Money is not everything, of course; you only need to have a nose for culture and a will to appreciate and to understand. So, equipped with these attributes, head back to the Farnese area to the street called **Via del Governo Vecchio** and its continuation, Via Banchi Nuovi. There you'll find, in

*Pavement artist at work*

the small, lively, secondhand clothes shops, in the smart cafés and cheap but stylish shops, proof that if art is culture, craft is basically good taste.

One spectacular example: in that street you find the cheapest yet best pizza in Rome. The street is full of students and the not-so-young chatting happily and waiting for tables at **Baffetto**. And pizza, as any Roman student will tell you, is neither art nor craft: pizza is a way of life.

Is interior design art or craft? Well, it should be considered art, since the best museums, in Rome and elsewhere, are very respectful of interior design in such great *palazzi* as the Borghese or the Pamphili. As you have Farnese for the tiles, so you have **Cassinah** as a world name in design, at Via del Babuino 100. Its exhibits present a stark, strong look that calls to mind the work of Le Corbusier. A few other interior-design showrooms are worth a visit, such as **Stildomus**, just a few yards away at Via del Babuino 54, and **Spazio Sette**, a showroom with three levels in the Palazzo Lazzaroni (Via Barberi 7) near Largo Argentina. Here is a fascinating display of practically everything that belongs in a house, from furniture to vases.

For glass, the best place again is along the Via del Babuino; **Venini**, at number 30, has beautiful shop windows and marvellous but expensive glass rivalled only in Venice.

The most famous name in modern ceramics is **Richard Ginori**, with a shop at Via Cola di Rienzo 223. Fabric and wallpapers have a long tradition to fall back on and it's not been forgotten. **Cesari** at Via del Babuino 16 is the place to go to if you are seeking the best furnishing fabrics.

**Croff Centro Casa**, a subsidiary of Rinascente at Via Tomacelli 137, is the most renowned place for fabrics, linen and classically elegant household design objects. They are similar to the products of Habitat and IKEA, expected to open in Rome shortly.

*Mercato delle Stampe*

**A stroll through the smart streets around Piazza di Spagna.**

**Piazza di Spagna** is Rome's best stage setting if you discount St Peter's Square. The **Spanish Steps** (built in 1725) rise above, leading to the French church of Trinità dei Monti. Named after the Spanish Embassy to the Holy See, jubilant with flowers in the long Roman spring, the steps were filled in the 18th century by good-looking men and women seeking work as artists' models.

From the square lead the three streets that provide the fashion windows for the greatly celebrated Italian couture (designed in Milan and produced elsewhere). Via del Babuino, Via dei Condotti and Via Borgognona are highly stylish and stylised and offer a dose of worldwide names. **Armani**, at Via del Babuino 102, and **Versace**, at Via Borgognona 29, the two rival maestros, compete with each other rather like Bernini and Borromini did four centuries ago. This kind of rivalry between opposing masters is constant in Rome's artistic circles. Other high-fashion names are here too, including the old, ineffable dresser of stars and royalty, **Valentino,** with a menswear store in neighbouring Via dei Condotti and a womenswear shop at Via Bocca di Leone 15.

The queen of cashmere, **Laura Biagiotti** (Via Borgognona 43), provides a uniquely feminine touch, much loved by women who want to be classy in a gentle way. Next door to her, at Via Borgognona 39, you'll find the **Fendi** sisters, specialising in smart shoes and bagss and understated accessories.

Shopping here takes money, yes, but as everybody who comes to these three streets knows, money is not sufficient in itself. In Via Condotti there are two **Gucci** shops – the name that is probably the most-copied in the world, with hundreds of small sweatshops from Taiwan to the back streets of Naples churning out replica bags and watches. Meanwhile the Gucci dynasty fights over the spoils of an old name in a very Renaissance kind of battle.

Beltrami's name in Via dei Condotti 19 is more subdued and possibly much closer to the real spirit of the Renaissance, producing handmade shoes and exquisitely produced leather goods that rival those of the Florentine tradition.

This area is so entrenched in class and tradition that when a big international maker of jeans tried to set up shop – with the help of a garish neon sign – it caused such outrage that the necessary permits were refused until strict 'aesthetic' standards were met. In the end, the jeans manufacturer gave up.

While shopping in this neighbourhood you should visit **Antico Caffè Greco** where

*The Italians' favourite*

in the last century everybody who was somebody went to be seen. Goethe was among the first in a long succession of artists, composers and writers, which continues to the present day. The café remains an elegant, if somewhat stilted, place.

If you are looking for artists, **Via Margutta** is a lovely peaceful street just off Piazza di Spagna (though a more avant-garde art scene is found in the Trastevere area). In spite of becoming over-popular with tourists, it manages to retain a lot of style. But can you really do the ultimate? That is, walk into a shop and buy a painting by a master? Even a minor painting? Even a minor master? Yes, if you can afford it, you can. And if you have knowledge, culture, taste, and that indefinable mixture of the three that Italians call 'gusto', you might be able to find a small masterpiece for a relatively small sum. **W. Apol-**

*Window-shopping is free*

**loni**, round the corner in Via del Babuino 132–4, is a respected dealer, with 17th-century paintings, silver, and furniture. A few paces away at No 67, **Cesare Lampronti** is the dealer to see for 16th- to 18th-century painters. It's worth checking what Italians call **Gab** (Granmercato Antiquario Babuino), at Via del Babuino 150, for silver, porcelain or glass from the 17th century onwards.

If all these shops on Via del Babuino are too pricey for your pocket, there are other options. One is to turn up at Via Margutta either at Christmas or in the spring when a fair is held, with affordable items. The second option is to go to Via del Pellegrino and Via dei Coronari, where with good fortune you might end up in a thrift shop that has a small Titian, a forgotten Reni, or even a Caravaggio. It has been known to happen before and it may even happen again.

You could also check out the bookshop **Libreria del Viaggiarore** in the middle of Via del Pellegrino itself. For other bookshops, the **Feltrinelli** nearby, in Piazza Argentina, offers a good choice of books in Italian and some in English. But for the best choice of English books you should go to Via della Vite, where there are two stores, to the **Lion's** bookshop at Via del Babuino 181 or the **Economy Book and Video Centre** in Via Torino 136, where they sell videos as well.

Finally, from the sublime to the ridiculous, don't overlook the shops around the **Piazza Vittorio Emanuele II** which is becoming almost a permanent flea market, with scores of stores run by immigrants from mostly East Asian and African countries. You'll find good cheap food there, too, and for erotic items go to the **Mas** department store, which may soon be closed but for the time being is probably the cheapest in all of Rome.

# EXCURSIONS

## 8. The Etruscan Trail

**To the northwest of Rome to the former Etruscan towns of Cerveteri and Tarquinia and the 2,300-year-old bridge at Vulci.**

*–Railway stations: Cerveteri and Tarquinia on the Rome to Pisa line; bus: ACOTRAL, departing from Lepanto (Line A). Vulci is accessible only by car plus a lengthy walk–*

This itinerary is an absolute must for the romantic traveller, for the history lover and, above all, for the lover of mystery and magic.

There's a book in Italian, *Miti, Riti, Magie e Misteri degli Etruschi*, which gives an account of these people who knew about their forthcoming end but didn't do anything to prevent it; who built cities of the dead that were larger than those of the living; and whose sorcerer king were said to be able to command lightning. (This reputation was so durable that long afterwards – in the 4th century AD when the barbarians were menacing Rome – their help was still solicited for this purpose.)

We still don't know from where the Etruscan first came and their writing is the only written code that modern philologists haven't cracked. We do know that they had an efficient agricultural system, rich game and fishing and a cuisine and style of food preparation whose sophistication can be seen on frescoes and bas reliefs.

*A refined civilisation*

Their dozen city states were rich, powerful and so secure that for centuries they didn't even need walls. The sorcerer king was a benign head of state, all-powerful but helped by the great aristocratic families who had specific civic duties towards slaves and the poor. Music accompanied all work from hunting and harvesting to the cooking of food. The people lived contentedly in thousands of caves that dot their forested lands in Tuscany and Lazio.

*Etruscan tomb at Cerveteri*

The Etruscans never waged war and it's still unknown why Veio, a powerful city of 100,000 with an army and theoretically impregnable walls, could be captured (it took a century, however) by an uncouth, barely-armed scruffy band of Romans. Why didn't they ask for help from their sister cities? No historian wants to believe that the Etruscans simply gave way to fatalism when they knew their time was up.

Their great iron mines produced the bronze tripods that were found everywhere in ancient Greece. The Etruscan fleet was a large one that ranged far and wide, exporting metal tools as far east as the Danube, north to France, west to Spain and south to Egypt.

Of the thousands upon thousands of big, bronze statues that graced Etruscan towns we are left with but two and – ironically – one is the She-wolf in the Capitol, the figure that celebrates the legendary birth of Rome. The other, called the *Chimera*, sits in a museum at Arezzo in Tuscany, and is a strangely complex hybrid, part feline, part serpent.

Most of the best Etruscan sculpture is now preserved in the Vatican museums (*see page 35*) and Villa Giulia (*see page 49*), much of it having been salvaged from the four Etruscan towns nearest to Rome. **Veio**, which fell in AD396, has yielded up an impressive statue of Apollo whose knowing, mysterious smile somewhat resembles that of the Gioconda.

The ancient town of Caere, now **Cerveteri**, produced the bulk of the pieces in Rome's museums, but there is still pottery and sarcophagi to be seen in Cerveteri's own little museum in a Renaissance palace called **Ruspoli** (9am–4pm in winter, and until 7pm in summer, closed Mondays, admission free).

Caere was a major commercial port spreading over 71km (44 miles) of coastline. From its three harbours it conducted considerable trade with the Greeks and Carthaginians.

ACOTRAL buses to Cerveteri run every hour from the Metro stop Lepanto (Line A), on the Via Lepanto. The trip takes 40 minutes.

From the town's main square another bus runs to the **Banditaccia necropolis** on the hill. The tombs here are made of great mounds of earth with carved stone bases, often bearing paintings of hunting and fishing scenes and frequently hinting at all kinds of esoteric, magical forces. The most famous, *tomba dei rilievi*, is protected by glass but others – such as *tomba dei capitali* and *tomba dei vasi Greci* – are more accessible. Everybody was buried in pretty much the same style as he/she lived and no two tombs are alike. There are said to be almost 40,000 of them in the area, many as yet uncovered although the *tombaroli*, illegal grave-diggers, continue their nefarious work.

Another Etruscan centre, **Tarquinia** (90km/56 miles from Rome on the busy Aurelia road, and equally easy to reach by bus from the Lepanto bus station), is a lovely, sleepy medieval town with at least three attractive churches (Santa Maria di Castello, San Francesco and San Pancrazio) and a museum located in the 15th-century *palazzo* of the Vitelleschi family in the centre of town. It closes at 2pm (and all day Monday) so you'll need to make an early start. The most impressive piece is a terracotta relief of a pair of winged horses but there are also numerous sarcophagi taken from the surrounding region and beautiful frescoes taken from other tombs.

*Hop on a bus*

(Such removals wouldn't happen these days because current thinking sensibly maintains that a piece of ancient art should remain *in situ* where obviously the work can be better understood and appreciated.) If the museum's top floor happens to be closed, the custodian will unlock it for you on request.

The admission ticket also allows access to the necropolis, a 15-minute walk from the museum and also closing at 2pm. There are thousands of tombs here, most of them closed and unexcavated and others behind glass. You'll not want to overlook the *tomba della baccanti* (the dancers) and the *tomba della caccia e della pesca* (hunting and fishing) and *tomba del triclino* which depicts reclining diners at a feast. Even people who don't know much about the Etruscans remember that they ate while lying down, a habit later copied by Romans, who slandered their predecessors as decadent and lascivious. It's obvious, though, by the state of the countryside, the way the cities were built, the perfect water and sewage systems – all things the Romans copied from them – that the Etruscans were extremely skilled and competent workers.

**Vulci** is the least accessible of the old Etruscan settlements and, as indicated, you'll need a car to get there. Take the Via Aurelia road towards Grossetto and watch for the Vulci signpost after passing

*Keeping a watchful eye*

**Montàlto di Castro**. About 9.5km (6 miles) further on you'll come across the 11th-century black stone fortress of **Ponte d'Abbadia** with a museum (9am–1pm and 2.30–4pm) housing relics from the immediate area.

Keep left after the bridge to walk to Old Vulci, scrambling down the grave-covered hill and crossing the stream. You'll pass the Cuccumella, an Entruscan hill grave that's 150m (492ft) in diameter and see the foundations of the high tower that once over-shadowed it.

From Tarquinia it's worth making a trip to **Tuscania** which has two magnificent cathedrals, one dating from the 13th century. When you're ready to relax you'll find some of Italy's loveliest beaches near **Alberese** (after heading through Orbetello and Talamon).

## 9. Tivoli's Villas

**Villa d'Este and the ruins of the emperor's Villa Adriana are both near the town of Tivoli, one hour's drive from Rome.**

*–ACOTRAL bus from the Rebibbia stop on Line A of the Metro. Also guided tours (American Express and others) –*

About 40km (25 miles) east of Rome, in gentle hills near Tivoli, are two aristocratic playgrounds, the **Villa d'Este** and the **Villa Adriana**, which, though created 14 centuries apart, have much in common. They are both wonderful examples of what abundant money and style can produce.

Early into his reign (113–138) the emperor Hadrian had already made his mark on the vast Roman empire with impressive public works, incuding a majestic arch in Athens and the long wall separating England from Scotland. Both still stand today, as do Rome's Castel Sant' Angelo (intended to be his mausoleum) and the magnificent Pantheon (which replaced Agrippa's earlier structure).

So Hadrian turned his attention to creating a suitable home/retreat for himself away from the capital, and as emperor he had the power and resources to build what really turned out to be a complete town. Much of Hadrian's 'villa' still stands, more than 1,800 years later, and the **Villa Adriana** (9am–dusk, closed Monday) is his greatest monument.

*Venus at Villa Adriana*

Not content with mere homes, hospitals, stables, barracks and thermal baths, he also reproduced on the 113-ha (280-acre) grounds several of his empire's famous landmarks – Thessaly's Vale of Tempe, for example, and what has been called a recreation of the Egyptian city of Canopus with its statue-lined canal leading to the **Temple of Serapis.** (Some of the statues, however, are

copies of the caryatids on Athens' Acropolis.) On a small hill at this end of the grounds is a fairly well-preserved **Temple of Apollo** and the rectangular-shaped **Torre di Roccabruna** which may have been an observatory.

The not-very-helpful signs in academese (and tiny type) are somewhat redeemed with engravings by Piranesi, the 18th-century equivalent of what today would be a documentary photographer. Piranesi's 2,000 engravings were published as *Views of Rome* in 1750, a book that has been endlessly reprinted.

It takes hours to satisfy one's wanderlust, admiring the shape and bulk of the huge walls which look sturdy enough to last for at least another 2,000 years. The main palace buildings, baths and so-called **Maritime Theatre** (a circular pond with a tiny villa on its island) are relatively well preserved.

*Rear view at Tivoli*

For centuries after his death this grand achievement of Hadrian mouldered undisturbed and largely unseen, especially after it was plundered by barbarian invaders, but during the Renaissance there was a revival of interest in the ancient sites. The princes of the church sought to emulate this glory – and they, too, had the money to indulge their extravagant tastes.

Shortly after his appointment as pope in 1503, Julius II turned to Donato Bramante for help in solving a design problem: Julius's art collection in the Villa Belvedere was inconveniently far from the papal palace – especially on cold wintry days.

Since arriving in Rome at the age of 65, Urbino-born Bramante had spent four years (according to diarist Giorgio Vasari) 'studiously measuring' the Villa Adriana and was by now considered an authority on the classical style. The design he produced for Pope Julius at the Vatican was said to have introduced 'a new concept of space and dominated the future course of garden architecture'. Sadly he died in 1514, his work still unfinished, but an able successor, Pirro Ligorio, was standing in the wings and completed the Villa Belvedere project. Like his predecessor, Lig-

*Venus in the Villa Adriana*

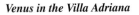

orio (1500–83) was also familiar with the Villa Adriana – he had compiled a portfolio of drawings of ancient sites – and by now, of course, was well-schooled in the Bramante style.

He especially admired the way the latter had dramatised the steep terrain with the use of monumental ramps and stairs, inking the hillside terraces. Thus in 1551 when he was commissioned to build a villa for Cardinal Ippolito d'Este, papal governor of Tivoli, Bramante's vision was much on his mind.

**Villa d'Este**'s (9.30am–dusk, closed Monday) cypress-filled, terraced gardens are indeed a dramatic sight: literally hundreds of fountains gushing from grottoes, statues and rocky clefts all subtly arranged so that whichever way one turns there is always more water around the next corner. The composer Liszt even named one of his compositions after the fountains (one of which, the *Fontana dell'Organo Idraulico*, actually did play music in its early days). Another of the fountains was designed by Bernini but even his work is surpassed by the staggering vista of the **Avenue of a Hundred Fountains** on the terrace below it.

Traversing the gardens involves a steep descent and a climb back up, but as long as your visit is well before sunset it can be done at a leisurely pace. There is a bar and restaurant on the terrace although prices are obviously higher than in the town of Tivoli.

## 10. The Castelli Romani

**One-hour's drive southeast of Rome takes you to the medieval village of Frascati, the pope's summer residence at Castel Gandolfo and the pagan shrine to the goddess Diana at Nemi.**

*–ACOTRAL buses (59, 55, 51) from Metro station Subaugusta on Line A–*

In the Alban Hills southeast of Rome the group of 13 towns known as the Castelli Romani all grew up around feudal castles. Today they are renowned the world over for their excellent food and wine. **Frascati**, the best known, is delightful and though located at least 160km (100 miles) from the sea prompted a turn-of-the-century writer to observe that 'one cannot help imagining the wash of waves instead of the grassy plain of the Campagna at the end of those coiling streets'.

*Swiss Guard at Castel Gandolfo*

Naturally, autumn is the best season to visit when the grape harvest is in full swing, but any time of the year is a good one to come and frequent the friendly taverns. Many good wine shops can be found along the **Via Regina Margherita** where some customers are in the habit of taking along their own food. (Tasty pieces of herb-stuffed suckling pig called *porchetta* is a regional favourite.)

Leaving the bus station, the park of the **Villa Torlonia** is just to the right. It offers panoramic views of the countryside but even more dramatic is the aspect from the **Villa Aldobrandi**, on the other side of the Via Cicerone. This was built for the nephew of Pope Clement VIII in 1602. As with the family's villa on Via Mazzanino in Rome, only the gardens are open to the public but their centrepiece is one of the most spectacular of all fountains.

The 18th-century English diarist John Evelyn was impressed not only by the fountain fed by a water staircase but by an 'elegant' garden that he felt surpassed 'the most delicious places that my eyes ever beheld.'

**Marino**, the nearest of the Castelli to Rome, is another place that attracts big crowds during the October grape harvest, partly on account of an old song that tells of the fountains that spill wine – a bit of poetic licence actually.

On the slopes of **Rocca Priora** is the Greek Orthodox abbey of **San Nilo**, famous for its own wine and for the splendid singing at its Sunday morning Mass. Also celebrated for its wine, and even more elevated, is **Rocca di Pappa** – 'the Pope's Rock' – on the northern slopes of of Monte Cavo, the highest peak (949m/3,114ft) of the Alban Hills.

The pope's actual summer residence is a few kilometres away in these hills at **Castel Gandolfo**, above the Lago di Albano. At this historic place popes have lived since 1624, but long before that it was famous as the site of Alba Longa, the city founded by Aeneas, the reputed father of Romulus and Remus.

The volcanic lake, some of which is 170m (558 ft) deep, is a popular spot in summertime for recreational boating. The occasional regattas plus the proximity of the pope in those months do wonders for the local tourist trade. The lake's overflow is handled by a tunnel 1.4km (almost a mile) long which was carved out of solid rock in 397BC and still does the job admirably.

The most peaceful and delightful of the Castelli villages is **Nemi** which in pre-Christian times was a pagan shrine devoted to the goddess of the hunt, Diana. Ruins of the ancient temple remain on the slopes between the village and the now polluted lake. This was drained in 1930 to recover two enormous boats (more than 70m/200ft long: 20m/65ft wide) built by the emperor Caligula (37–41) which proved helpful to historians in learning about ancient boat-building techniques. Unfortunately they were destroyed during World War II and although replicas were constructed and placed in the lakeside museum, this has been closed for many years.

If you are driving, **Palestrina** makes for an interesting stop-off on the way back to Rome. An ancient Etruscan town with many ruins, it has been a favourite retreat for affluent residents of the capital since the days of the early emperors. Reputedly founded by Telegonos, the son of Odysseus, it was originally called Praeneste. When the 1st-century lyric poet Horace, who had a villa in nearby Tivoli, described it as 'cool', he was undoubtedly referring to the climate. There are still impressive remains of the shrine of **Fortuna Primigenia** where the goddess of fortune was worshipped. Among her later patrons were members of two patrician Roman families, the Colonnas and the Barberinis, whose palaces were built into part of the temple itself.

This is now a museum (Museo Nazionale Archaeologico Prenestino) on the top floor of which is the quite extraordinary Nile Mosaic, at least 2,000 years old, which shows the valley of the Nile teeming with life. One of the shrine's main attractions in ancient time was the oracle, mentioned in the writings of Cicero.

The little town, enclosed within the temple's extensive walls, is a mecca for admirers of the local mushroom, *funghi porcini*, which for centuries has been a rare delicacy. After the 16th century the town changed its name to honour its native son Giovanni Perluigi di Palestrina, born here in 1525, whose distinguished musical career as a composer included many years as organist and choirmaster at St Peter's in Rome.

*The Nile Mosaic, Palestrina*

*Ostia's amphitheatre*

## 11. Ostia Antica

**The ancient port of Rome can be reached via Metro Line A from Piramides station, changing at Magliana to the Lido di Ostia train (same ticket) to Ostia Antica. On arrival cross all the highways, and keep straight ahead.**

Your best choice for a short excursion is the ancient seaport of **Ostia Antica** which can be reached from Rome within an hour but will keep you fascinated until it closes an hour before sunset. Take along food and drink because there is none at the site and you'll enjoy having lunch with a fallen marble column as your picnic table.

*Roman mosaic*

Ostia Antica is among the best preserved of all ancient Roman cities, largely because it gradually slid from being a bustling port into a rural backwater and eventually became covered by sand and forgotten for centuries.

The earliest town wall went up in 335BC with the sea protecting the city at the western side. Sitting at the mouth of the Tiber, it was the first landfall for all the treasures bound for Rome from the far-flung corners of the empire. The shipping business was an especially lucrative one with its importers and exporters, timber merchants and boat-builders, sail and rope-makers.

From the earliest days, the silt brought by the river caused a problem for the navy; Augustus moved the naval base down the coast, but Ostia continued to flourish as the port at which grain from Africa was unloaded. After Claudius (41–54) and then Trajan (98–117) dredged the harbour and rebuilt the docks, the port continued to grow steadily and by the late 2nd century its population exceeded 100,000.

In the 2nd century a new port was built further up the coast and gradually the life-blood of Ostia began to ebb away, later hastened by pirate raids and malaria from the untended and expanding marshes.

After the 4th century it was deserted and forgotten – which is what makes it such a superlative time-trip for today's visitors.

As you stroll down the main street, **Decimanus Maximus**, it is not hard to visualise the scurrying figures who once thronged this roughly-paved thoroughfare passing in and out of these very same stores and offices whose empty shells still line each side. Here and there a pillar still stands or the counter and shelves of a tavern, the stone ovens of a bakery. The mosaic of a fish indicates what was sold in one store; black and white tiles depicting wrestlers identify an athletic academy.

Discreet bilingual signs identify most things of interest – and there is plenty of it. A large **amphitheatre** with 3,000 seats is virtually intact. At the crossroads where the broad main street and the winding road to the river intersect, a small shrine was erected to mark the siting of this auspicious junction. Temples abound. The biggest are those at either end of the vast **forum**, the **Capitolium** with steps as impressive as in any 20th-century capital city, and the **Temple of Rome and Augustus**, built by Tiberius.

Behind the forum were the big public baths, not too far from the well-preserved **Casa di Diana**, a three-storey block of flats which shared a central courtyard with fountain, just around the corner from the bakery.

Behind the theatre was the **Piazza della Corporazione** where the big shippers and traders had their offices. There were at least 60 of these and it's worth walking over there to inspect some of their ancient 'trademarks' and the mosaics depicting scenes of busy city life. The River Tiber ran right by the piazza in those days (it has since slightly changed its course) and it is not difficult to picture the tycoons leaning from their windows on that exciting day in AD45 when Cleopatra's regal barge passed by, heading upriver for her rendezvous with Julius Caesar in Rome.

On your way back to the station you'll see the **castle** which was built in 1483 by Baccio Pontelli, regarded as one of the best examples of Renaissance fortifications. Its round tower looks over a moat. Inside, what was once an apartment for the pope is now a small museum and there are interesting frescoes on the main staircase by Baldassare Peruzzi who was also responsible for the nearby Sant' Aurea church.

The present-day city of Ostia has little to interest tourists. Even the beaches in summer are more decorative than useful, for the water is too polluted for bathing. There is a 'secret' nudist beach called Il Buco, 'the hole', because access is via a hole in the fence. If you choose to get back on the train after visiting Ostia Antica you'll discover, when you arrive at **Lido di Ostia**, that the sea is still a long walk from the station. There is, however, a well-stocked supermarket on the right of the piazza.

*Mosaic detail, Ostia Antica*

# Eating Out

## Pizzerias and Trattorias

Romans call them *pizza al taglio*. They are small, colourful places found everywhere, with hot pizzas served in rectangular shapes of any size you want (you pay according to weight). Sometimes there are tables in these places, but not often, for most customers wolf the food down while standing. Pizza parlours, where you sit down, serve the familiar big, round pizzas with a wide and sometimes wild range of toppings: tomatoes, potatoes, aubergines and their flowers, zucchini and almost any other vegetables you can think of, as well as various meats, ham or fish. White wine is the best companion to Roman pizza, but beer goes well too.

Trattorias serve Roman food which is rather heavy: lots of oil and meat with rich sauces. Your pasta might be the long kind (*spaghetti*) or the short kind (*rigatoni*, *pasta corta*, *bucatini*) and your sauce *aglio e olio* (oil and garlic: the simplest), *amatriciana* (spicy tomato sauce and bacon) or *carbonara* (bacon, egg yolk, pepper and Parmesan or *pecorino* cheese). You may want to try *penne all'arrabiata*, a short kind of pasta with strong *peperoncino* making it very hot.

Your second course will be meat or fish. There's the usual beef steak and pork chops but also what has traditionally been served over the years to the less affluent, the cheaper cuts of meat and offal, including *trippa* (tripe), *cervello* (brains), *rognoncino* (sliced kidneys), *agnello* (lamb) and *abbacchio* (mutton), with different kinds of sauces. Classic trattoria fare is *saltimbocca alla romana* (a slice of *proscuitto* and a leaf of fresh sage rolled up with a thin slice of veal, then browned in butter and simmered in white wine).

Around Piazza di Spagna, the nameless place at Via Margutta 82 (tel: 320-7713) serves good food for a reasonable £10–18 in an expensive part of town. At the corner of Corso and Via Condotti, at Via del Leoncino 28, is the **Pizzeria Il Leoncino** (tel: 687-6306) where good pizza costs about £7 including wine. If you want to plunge into the world of Italian journalists and politicians, you'll often find them eating at **Gino** (Vicolo Rossini 4) where you'll enjoy tasty cuisine for around £10–12. It's located in a lovely, old-town area between the Pantheon and the Parliament.

At Piazza Pasquino 73, is the **Cul de Sac**, a wine bar with light meals starting around £10. Nearby, still in the Piazza Navona area, is the maybe too famous **Baffetto** (Governo Vecchio 11), popular mostly with students who like to try out their English on strangers. Pizzas here are good as well as cheap, and there are outdoor tables. Further down the street at **No 18** is another trattoria with no name and also no menu. Serving good Roman food, it is run by Antonio Bassetti, who will explain everything to you if you are patient.

This street changes its name further down, becoming Via Banchi Nuovo. At **No 14** is a small trattoria run by Alfred and Ada, an elderly couple who have been serving up simple but delicious meals for half a century. You eat what's offered, with no choice, just like it was in the 1950s: a £10 trip into a Rome trattoria of yesteryear.

In Campo dei Fiori there's **Hostaria Romanesca** with outdoor tables, where you will find good food for £10–15 in a superlative setting. Heading off the Campo along Via dei Giubbonari and on to Largo dei Librari, you'll come across **Filetti di Baccala** (tel: 686-4018), which serves only deep-fried cod fillets and wine. At the end of that street, cross Via Arenula and you'll be in the Jewish area where **Sora Margherita** (Piazza delle Cinque Scole, tel: 686-4002) offers a traditional Jewish-Roman cuisine: a simple place with inexpensive prices – around £10 for a full meal.

*A city for eating out*

*Markets are the best source of fresh produce*

Across the river in Trastevere are dozens of restaurants – you're best off just wandering randomly – but some of them are difficult to find in the maze of small streets (for a restaurant tour of Trastevere, *see page 32*). **Augusto** (Piazza de Renzi 15), in a lovely square that is unfortunately heavily infested with cars, serves good, earthy food and attracts an interesting mixture of locals and foreigners mingling at the outdoor tables. Another popular pizzeria, just off this square, is **Ivo** (Via San Francesco a Ripa 158, tel: 581-17082), whose large outdoor tables are useful when there are several people in your party.

## Restaurants

Of course, there is not just Roman cuisine available but many different regional variations from all over Italy. Tuscan, very classic,

is probably the most popular alternative, and **Mario** (Via della Vite 55, tel: 678-3818), off Piazza di Spagna, is a good but fairly expensive dispenser of this style of cuisine (around £20 and up).

The best-known restaurant in the Piazza di Spagna area is **Dal Bolognese**, next to the Rosati café in Piazza del Popolo. It is high-class, more than a touch touristy and the sort of place where people go to see and be seen. This slice of Roman chicness will run you up a bill of around £35 for dinner.

A good traditional restaurant close to the Trevi Fountain is **Al Moro** (Vicolo delle Bollette 13, tel: 678-3495): full dinner will cost around £20 a head.

**Fortunato al Pantheon** (tel: 679-2788) is, of course, close to the famous landmark at Via del Pantheon 55. It's patronised by politicians, has outdoor tables that can be booked in summer, and costs about £20–30 a head for dinner.

Also in this neighbourhood is the oldest restaurant in Rome, **La Campana** (Vicolo della Campana 18, tel: 686-7820), which is perennially popular and deserving of its fame (about £20 a head).

**Il Cardinale** (Via delle Carceri 6, off Via Giulia) has first-rate food and runs to a little more, as does **La Tana dei Noantri** (Via dell Paglia 1, tel: 580-6404) in a charming setting just off Piazza Santa Maria in Trastevere.

## Ethnic Restaurants

Somewhat belatedly, Rome is becoming an international city and its cuisine is broadening at the same pace. In addition to the 200 or more Chinese restaurants that have opened in the past few years there are scores of others presenting foods of many differing cultures. Indian restaurants in particular have proliferated, offering a very good meal for the price. **India House** (Via Santa Cecilia 8 in Trastevere, tel: 581-8508) is the best of these: set menus, both vegetarian and otherwise, for around £14. Another one, slightly more expensive, **Suria Mahal** (Via Ponte Sisto 67, tel: 589-4554), enjoys a grandiose setting, just behind the Piazza Trilussa fountain (you'll need to make a reservation). The truly exquisite one, however, is **Himalaya's Kashmir** (Via Principe Amedeo 325, tel: 446-4906), off Piazza Vittorio Emanuele. It's well worth the £18 or so per head for Indo-Pakistani specialities.

Off this same Piazza Vittorio, near Termini station, is **Ristorante Mar Rosso** (Via Conte Verde 62, tel: 446-4495) which serves up a set menu of African food, the usual chapati bread-pancake with spicy mutton (about £10-14) which should be tackled with your hands. Similar cuisine can be enjoyed at **Sahara** (Viale Ippocrate 43, tel: 442-42583), an Eritrean establishment with a big terrace and delicious honey wine to go with your meal. Another good experience can be **Messico e Nuvole** (Via dei Magazzini Generali 8, tel: 574-1413), which offers spicy Mexican food and a lively atmosphere, especially enjoyable during good weather when you can eat on the terrace. The £20 or so per head is well spent.

**Note:** The prices listed are only a rough guide because what you pay obviously depends on what you order. The prices here refer to a full meal with local or house wine.

As a general rule, but with many exceptions, trattorias shut on Sundays and restaurants on Mondays. Most establishments will serve food until about 3pm, when they close until about 7pm and then re-open for the evening. Trattorias close early at 10pm, and restaurants at 11pm or midnight. Only a very few stay open later. With occasional exceptions, you can sit outdoors and eat from April to October in Rome.

*Waiting for the rush*

# Nightlife

'La Dolce Vita', Rome's famous good life, is still here all right, but not in the Via Veneto any more. Now *la dolce vita* centres on Trastevere with another portion of it in the area known as 'the Bermuda triangle', just off Piazza Navona, and some in the Testaccio area around Monte dei Cocci (a 3rd-century BC rubbish dump).

Remember that Rome has two distinct seasons, the indoor one lasting from November to March (although there are days even in January when you can sit outside) and the outdoors season beginning, with luck, in April and lasting until autumn. The current place to go, **Gilda** (Via Mario de' Fiori 97), now has **Gilda on the Beach** at Fregene, a nearby seaside resort that opens for summer only.

The **Trastevere** scene comprises restaurants, wine bars and beer places, small clubs of all kinds – sometimes with live music, more often 'canned' – or just tiny places to flirt and talk. The young hang out in the pizza and beer spots, the not-so-young in the wine bars. At 1am it all closes down.

The **Piazza Navona** nightlife scene can be found by taking the small street leading from the sedate, touristy Tre Scalini bar and following the scene as it unfolds, spilling in and out of various spots. It's probably more enjoyable if you go with a local who understands it but in any case it continues until two or three in the morning.

The **Testaccio** scene (ask your taxi driver to take you to 'Il Mattatoio', the slaughter house, and start roving) begins around 11pm, lasts all night and attracts a wilder kind of night owl, including the transvestite crowd. 'Trans', as they are known mostly, come

from Brazil and are beautiful creatures of the night who sell (for £15–35) the most unashamed sex in town. Most of them have impossibly long legs, silicon breasts and the great metaphysical surprise (to some) that under those vertiginous miniskirts is a male member. The whole scene, though not for the prudish, is entertaining to observe.

*Take two girls*

*The Spanish Steps by night*

After a decade of boredom, something rather fascinating is happening to Rome's nightlife, partly due to an astonishing influx of people of the night from all parts of the globe. Once they came to the imperial city as slaves, now they come from the slavery of poverty in their home countries in Africa, Asia, the East and South America. It has created a bubbling cauldron of cultures, a melting pot of wildly different people reflected very strikingly in ethnic restaurants and ethnic music. While Paris and London were flooded with immigrants from their colonies and gradually absorbed them, in Rome the invasion has only recently begun and there's a dizzying excitement in the air. Don't come here if

you disapprove or think it's too sinful or too rough, but it's so close to ancient Rome, both geographically and sociologically, that the locals find it fascinating.

## Practical Tips

*La Repubblica*'s supplement 'Trovaroma' lists everything – music and theatre, sports and movies, along with addresses, telephone numbers and schedules. It's in Italian but names and times are the same in every language.

Romans don't book for anything except the opera and some theatre; it's against their nature to do anything but just turn up and take their chance. But you can book, if you like, tel: 372-0215 (the box office number for a lot of things). On an evening out be prepared to pay at least L10,000, drinks included. Some rock, disco, jazz (very good in Rome), classical music and dance performances may be even more.

Listings can also be found in the two English-language publications *Wanted in Rome* and *Metropolitan*.

## Classical Music and Dance

You will come across choral performances in churches everywhere. The big places for serious music are the **Santa Cecilia auditorium**, the **Foro Italico** and the **Teatro dell'Opera**. Summer brings outdoor concerts, including a festival at the Caracalla Baths. In July, there are concerts in the grounds of Villa Giulia and the cloisters of Santa Maria della Pace. Summer orchestral concerts take place around the **Teatro di Marcello** and at the **Villa Pamphili** and **Pincio Gardens**. Classical music in such glorious settings brings many people to Rome especially to hear it.

## Rock, Jazz, Folk Music

Big rock concerts are held at the **Palazzetto dello Sport**, a covered arena holding 20,000, and at open soccer stadiums holding around 60,000. On a smaller scale, two places in the Testaccio area are **Il Mattatoio** and **Villaggio Globale**, which offer African, Asian, Italian, whatever. Turn up early. **Uonna** (Via Cassia 871), the in-place in the 1970s, is still going strong offering hard rock, trash, punk, reggae, rap. You must be a member (you can become one at the door) and it's an expensive taxi ride (about £10) from the centre. Near Campo dei Fiori is **Osiris** (Largo dei Librari) with rock, pop, mainstream and even the occasional poetry reading.

Out of the way but worth seeking out is **Forte Frenestino**, a splendid fort occupied by politically-minded squatters, where occasional rock concerts are held in a unique setting. **Alpheus** (Via del Commercio 36) offers different kinds of music all in the same building. It includes jazz, as does **Il Castello** and lots of smaller places such as **Mississippi Blues**, **Saint Louis Music City** (Via del Cardello

13), **Ciao Musica** and **Caffè Les Folies**, some of them clubs and some pubs and none with regular schedules. Rome's temple of folk music is **Folkstudio** in Trastevere which started in the early 1960s with Giancarlo Cesaroni. Check also the new **Shamrock**, in the Colosseum area, and **Fonklea** (where you can also eat) around St Peter. Irish folk music is currently popular in Rome, along with American.

*One of many options*

## Movies, Theatre, Opera, Dance

Only one cinema, the **Pasquino** (Vicolo del Piede, Trastevere) shows a different English-language movie every day, and you must book your seat beforehand, although the same evening is soon enough. Nearby is the **Alcatraz**, small, smart and snobbish, that shows English-language movies on Monday.

An interesting possibility you might want to explore is the cineclubs which show original versions of movie classics. The best of them is **Azzurro Scipioni** (Via Scipione 84, tel: 397-37161) in the Vatican area. It puts on six movies a day in its twin theatres (at 6.30, 8.30 and 10.30pm) and the £5 entrance fee allows admission to everything. Both theatres are small and cosy and operated in a charming way by an Italian director, Silvano Agosti, and his family. Another good one is **Nuovo Sacher** (in Trastevere) which is run by the famous Italian director Nanni Moretti. This is a haunt of movie buffs and the intelligentsia. It has a bar, books and movies on sale and moves outdoors during the summer.

As for theatre, there are frequent visits by English companies with outdoor performances at the tiny **Quercia del Tasso**, at the

*Transvestite club*

top of the Gianicolo Hill, and **Ostia Antica** (*see page 72*), where performances take place in the old Roman amphitheatre. Both can be inspiring experiences.

Opera in Rome has two seasons: from November to January at the **Teatro dell'Opera** and the summer one at the **Caracalla Baths**. Reservations necessary for both of these, of course.

## Other Nightlife

**Piper 90** (Via Tagliamento 9) is the oldest and most famous rock/disco place and it also has a video theatre.

English-speaking locals gravitate towards the **Blu Bar** (Via dei Soldati 25) and the **Little Bar** (Via Gregoriana 54a), but for some time the trendiest place in town has been the **Hemingway** (an American bar in Roman style) followed closely by the **Zelig**. Also in the running are **Caffè della Pace**, on the street of that name, and **Le Cornacchie**, (Piazza Ronadini 53) both near Piazza Navona. **Gilda** is a jet-set haven; **Jackie O**, on the other hand, is for people with more money than style.

**Open Gate**, **Notorius** and **Divina** are all trendily fashionable places and none of them is cheap; expect to go through £75 in a night, maybe only £30 if you're really careful.

The hottest club for young people is probably the **Alien** (Via Velletri 13) while **Soul II Soul** (Via dei Fienaroli 30a, Trastevere) has a very mixed black and white crowd. **Circolo degli Artisti** (Via Lamarmora 28, near the station) stages avant-garde concerts from around Europe and **Blue Zone** (Via Campania 37a) and **Le Stelle** (Via C. Beccaria 22) are a couple of smart places that warm up around 3am and keep going until dawn. The **Maghreb** (Piazza Cestia, by the Pyramid) is a lively African restaurant which also has music.

The gay night scene in Rome is very active, with **Alibi** (Via di Monte Testaccio 44) being the most famous spot. **Angelo Azzurro** (Via Card. Merry del Val 13) is also the centre of a lively scene. You could begin your evening at a bar called **Hangar** (Via in Selci 69) and simply keep your ears open for what's happening that night. Women might find companions at **Panico** (Via di Panico 13) on Sundays and at **Galaxia** (Piazza Bulgarelli 41) on Fridays and Sundays.

*Trastevere at night*

# Practical Information

## GETTING THERE

### By Air

There are direct scheduled flights to Rome from most major European cities, from Australia and from a number of cities in North America. From many European countries, there are also charter flights.

Travellers on scheduled flights land at the main airport, Aeroporto Leonardo da Vinci in Fiumicino, about 30km (18 miles) southwest of Rome (**Fiumicino airport**,

tel: 65951). Charters come into Ciampino airport, about 15km (9 miles) to the southeast (**Ciampino airport**, tel: 794941).

### By Rail

There are train services to Rome from all over Italy and from northern Europe.
If you are travelling from the UK, bear in mind that the cost of a train ticket is likely to be approximately the same as the airfare, and it is therefore only worth travelling by train if you intend to stop off along the way.

Most train travellers arrive at the main Roman station, Termini. Motorail trains come into the Stazione Tiburtina to the northeast of the centre, as do some trains on the north-south line (Bologna, Florence, Naples).

### By Coach

If you are travelling by coach, you will almost certainly arrive at or near the Stazione Termini. Most of the European coach companies as well as the Italian ones (Lazzi Express, Appian Line, ACOTRAL) use the Piazza dei Cinquecento as their terminus.

### By Road

Car travellers arriving in Rome from all directions first hit the Gran Raccordo Anulare (abbreviated GRA), the ring motorway. The A1 'Autostrada del Sole' leads into the GRA from both north and south as does the A24 from the east. If you arrive on the Via del Mare from the coast (Ostia), you can either switch on to the GRA or simply continue straight into the centre of the city.

The various roads into the centre lead off the GRA. It is best to study the map and choose your exit according to the part of the city you are heading for. For the northern area, choose the exits Via Salaria, Via Flaminia or Via Nomentana. If heading for the Vatican area, follow the GRA to the west and take the exit Via Aurelia. For the south, take the Via Tuscolana, Via Appia Nuova, Via Pontina (which leads into the Via Cristoforo Colombo) or the Via del Mare.

When leaving the GRA, you should follow white signs for the road you want rather than blue: the blue ones usually

lead away from the centre. Look also for the city centre sign: a black point in the middle of a black circle on a white background.

## TRAVEL ESSENTIALS

### Climate

Average daytime temperatures in Rome: Jan: 7.5°C (46°F); Feb: 8.8°C (48°F); Mar: 10.8°C (51°F); Apr: 14.2°C (58°F); May: 18.2°C (65°F); June: 22.3°C (72°F); July: 24.9°C (77°F); Aug: 24.6°C (76°F); Sept: 21.3°C (70°F); Oct: 16.8°C (62°F); Nov: 12.8°C (55°F); Dec: 8.7°C (48°F). Lows in January/February can reach 0°C (32°F), while highs in August sometimes exceed 35°C (95°F).

### When to Visit

Try to come to Rome in the spring or autumn. In winter you'll have the major sites all to yourself but you can get cold and wet. July is pleasantly warm, but already crowded; August more so as well as hot and humid and many shops are closed then (you might. however, find the near-deserted city to your taste). From mid-July to roughly mid-September the traditional festival called *Estate Romana* takes place, with movies and music in lovely open-air settings, close to or in historical sites.

### Clothing

Rome is a fairly formal city so shorts and T-shirts are looked at askance, except on the beach, and casual wear is definitely discouraged, not only in the Vatican but

*Hailing a cab*

### Killing two birds with one stone

in all churches, where long trousers and long sleeves for both men and women are expected. Incidentally, wearing a money belt is much safer than carrying a bag.

## MONEY MATTERS

You'll need Italian lire to leave the airport or the station so either bring some or get change as soon as possible. Most credit cards are accepted by restaurants and shops but you'll need cash for transport, bars, museum tickets, etc. Banks are open weekdays 8.30am–1.30pm and 2.45–3.45pm. For preference choose mainstream banks or exchange offices that display 'No Commission' signs (commission can sometimes be 4 percent or more). Machines that change foreign currency are often found near historical landmarks (such as the Pantheon). At Fiumicino and Termini there are change offices open until 7.30pm (closed Sundays).

## GETTING AROUND

### Airport Connections

From Fiumicino airport, trains run to the central stations Ostiense and Termini. If you must take a taxi choose only a yellow or white one with a meter. Other choices can be both expensive and dangerous. Be prepared for a taxi fare of £25–40 to your hotel from Fiumicino; £6–15 to your hotel from Termini or Ostiense.

Tel: 3750 or 4994 for radio taxis.

### Taxis, Buses, Trams and Metro

Driving in Rome is definitely not recommended and walking would be a delight were it not for the traffic. Successive governments,intimidated by a short-sighted

*Porta San Sebastiano*

## Trains

When you want to leave town by rail you will find Termini station a frustrating experience with long waits at the enquiries desk (and to buy tickets). You will get better, more reliable service from most travel agencies and, in particular, from the efficient American Express office on the Piazza di Spagna.

## Driving

Using a car in Rome's tangled streets can be an exercise in frustration. If you are driving around Italy it is advisable to check the car into a garage for your stay in the capital. However, it is useful to know that the state tourist office offers discount coupons subsidising the cost of petrol. Ask your home country's automobile club for details of how to obtain *Pachetto Italia*, which is a packet of these coupons.

Rental cars are available from Hertz (tel: 463-334), Maggiore (858-698), Avis (47011) Europcar (475-0381) and Eurodrive (460-920). For information about road conditions, tel: 4212.

shopkeepers' lobby, have failed to keep traffic out of even the narrowest streets so what you'll remember most about your stay is constantly jumping out of the way of cars and motorcycles. Nevertheless, walking is by far the best way to see the city centre, and especially Trastevere.

Yellow and white taxis begin their meters at around L6500, with a short trip costing £3.50 or so, a medium one, £6. After 10pm there is an additional night surcharge. Pay only what's on the meter plus 5 percent tip. Taxis get stuck, like buses, in traffic jams at any time of the day.

Tobacco stores displaying a big, black T sell bus tickets, without which you are not supposed to board a bus. There's a fine if you're caught without a ticket or without having stamped it in the machines close to the rear door. Watch your bag and your pockets to guard against purse-snatchers and pickpockets.

Bus-stops have yellow metal displays with routes, and a red circle around the place you're at; very clear and simple. Bus lines (and some trains) are operated by ACOTRAL (tel: 5915551) and a complete list of bus and tram lines can be obtained from the ATAC booth in Piazza dei Cinquecentro, opposite Termini station. A three-hour sightseeing bus tour leaves Termini at 3.30pm every day in summer, on weekends in winter.

The Metro is a skeletal system with only two lines, A and B, which intersect at Termini. Except for going to the seaside it is not very useful for tourists although Line B does connect Termini and Piramides stations. the latter being where you catch the train to Ostia (change at Magliana) and also the best place to catch the No 28 bus to Trastevere.

*Dodging the traffic*

## HOURS & HOLIDAYS

### Official Holidays

**1 January** New Year's Day
**6 January** Epiphany
**Easter**
**25 April** Liberation Day
**1 May**
**Whit Sunday** (Monday not a holiday)
**15 August** The Assumption of Mary
**1 November** All Souls' Day
**8 December** Feast of the Immaculate Conception
**25–26 December** Christmas

## Holidays and Festivals

New Year's Eve is very big business in Rome: drinking, dancing, noisy midnight celebrations with firecrackers and people throwing plates and other items out of windows. New Year is in the middle of a long holiday period that starts the day before Christmas when school shuts, and lasts until Epiphany on 6 January. Some families leave the city, many to their home villages. Young singles seek out faraway sunny places or nearby ski resorts. The days before Christmas are filled with frantic buying; the days after with sales and bargains. Those staying in Rome usually visit the annual Christmas Market in Piazza Navona which runs through the whole of December

Easter is usually a three- or four-day holiday. Italians say Christmas you spend with your family, Easter with whomever you want. Many head for St Peter's Square at noon on Easter Sunday for the pope's traditional *urbi-et-orbi* blessing. The saints' days of St Joseph (19 March) and St John (23 June) are celebrated with special dishes, and on Good Friday there's a procession from the Palatine to the Colosseum.

The town empties in August. Roman families head for the sea, north or south according to budget, class and where their second home might be. One family in three has a home at the seaside or in the village from which they came. Rome is a city whose population has exploded over the past 50 years, with new arrivals mostly from southern Italy. When people leave for their second homes on weekends, the city is noticeably less hectic, less noisy and less crowded. Take advantage of this.

## Opening Times

Most little shops and bars follow the traditional 'split' day, opening at 8 or 9am until about 1pm, then closing for a few hours to re-open later at about 3.30 or 4pm. Almost all are closed on Sundays and many don't open until late afternoon on Mondays. Restaurants, of course, are an exception to this.

Unfortunately, most museums also follow the custom of closing in the middle of the day and some do not re-open until the next day so check before making your plans. In the smarter, touristy shopping areas, shops open around 9 or 9.30am and remain open 'non-stop' until late in the evening. However, Italians are not familiar with the 24-hour concept and it is rare to come across a shop open very late at night.

*Late-night snack merchant*

## ACCOMMODATION

Try for a hotel as near as possible to the city centre; you'll be saving time, taxi fares and a lot of energy because in Rome you'll want to walk a lot. The best areas are around the smart Piazza del Popolo or Piazza Navona. The district around the Termini station is snarling with traffic and rather seedy.

If you really want to 'live like the Romans', plunge into the town and feel it, both the ancient and contemporary, you are advised to stay in an area near the great monuments of ancient Rome. You might be a student or budget traveller, somebody happy with a cheap and spartan room, or you may want the elegant ambience of a good room with a private bath and TV. You might even desire a luxurious, well-serviced hotel, and money will have a lot to do with your choice. But when you walk out of your hotel, if

*A characterful place to lodge*

you find yourself in front of the Pantheon or Piazza di Spagna or Navona, or in one of the narrow, medieval streets that lead to one of the classical squares, you'll really *know* you're in Rome.

The perfect example is the **Hotel Abruzzi** (Piazza della Rotonda 69, tel: 679-2021), an old hotel directly overlooking the Pantheon and yet in the £40–50 range. Three doors away is the **Sole al Pantheon** (Via del Pantheon 63, tel: 678-0441) with the same impressive view but for a price of £150–200. At the latter you'll be staying in a hotel opened in 1467 in which Renaissance poets, artists and prominent figures have stayed over the centuries, right up to Sartre in the 1960s. You can have a room with painted, panelled ceilings and a Jacuzzi.

Another simple, cheap place in a near-perfect location is the **Hotel Navona** (Via dei Sediari 18, tel: 686-4203) which is just off the famous square and has rooms with bath and without; £33–40. Nearby is another contrast, the **Raphael** (Largo Febo 2, tel: 650-8852), luxury without pomp and filled with sculptures both ancient and modern. Rates begin at about £130 and include breakfast.

Over by Trajan's Markets, in a quiet street and with a fine view from its balconies, is the **Forum** (Via Tor de Conti 28, tel: 679-2446) whose relatively high tariff (around £130) can be well worth the expense.

In the following list, price code: (**£** = up to £50, **££** = £50–100, **£££** = £100–180, **££££** = over £180) refer to the lowest price of a double room with private facilities (where available).

## Piazza di Spagna area

**HASSLER**
*Piazza Trinita dei Monti 6.*
*Tel: 678-2651*
Top of its class and atop the Spanish Steps. Bedrooms with Venetian glass chandeliers, marble bathrooms, and elegant rooftop restaurant. **££££**

**INGHILTERRA**
*Via Bocca di Leone 14*
*Tel: 672-161*
Opened in 1850 and host to Hemingway and many other writers, artists and musicians who adore its clubby English ambience. **££££**

**SCALINATA DI SPAGNA**
*Piazza Trinita dei Monti 17*
*Tel: 679-3006*
A 19th-century hotel in a great location, right at the top of the Spanish Steps. **£££**

**MARGUTTA**
*Via Laurina 34*
*Tel: 679-8440*
In a quiet street just off Piazza del Popolo, its best rooms are at the top sharing a roof terrace. Book well in advance. **££**

**JONELLA**
*Via della Croce 41*
*Tel: 679-7966*
Tiny with nine, slightly tarnished but comfortable rooms. **£**

## Campo dei Fiori area

Some of the small hotels around here have been sheltering pilgrims since the Middle Ages. It's still a free and easy marketplace with streets named after ancient trades (*Giubbonari* means jacket makers; *Chiavari* means nail makers, *Cappellari* means hatmakers) which are still practised in countless ground floor *bottegas*.

**DELLA LUNETTA**
*Piazza del Paradiso 68*
*Tel: 686-1080*
Situated in an old but interesting square, this 36-room hotel has rooms with and without bath. **£**

### PICCOLO
*Via dei Chiavari 32*
*Tel: 654-2560*
An old favourite with seasoned travellers.
Small, fairly cheap and reliable. **£**

### RINASCIMENTO
*Via del Pellegrino 122*
*Tel: 687-4813*
Centrally located in a street with three
book-stores, one specialising in travel. **££**

### SMERALDO
*Vivolo dei Chiarodoli 11*
*Tel: 687-5929*
The garish entrance belies this simple, 35-
room hotel which fills up early. **££**

### SOLE
*Via del Biscione 76*
*Tel: 688-06873*
Centuries-old with charming character and
its own garden, this quiet haven is often
booked up so call well ahead of your visit
to be sure of a room. **££**

### CAMPO DE FIORI
*Via del Biscione 6*
*Tel: 654-0865*
Lovely small hotel that's well located. **£££**

## Trastevere area

### CARMEL
*Via Mameli 11*
*Tel: 580-9921*
Six bathless but spotless rooms. Children
unwelcome. **£**

### MANARA
*Via Manara 23*
*Tel: 581-4713*
Close to the heart of Trastevere but fairly
unknown. Spartan and cheap, with half
a dozen rooms. **£**

## Vatican area

### ALIMANDI
*Via Tunisi 8*
*Tel: 397-23948*
A simple *pensione* situated very close to
St Peter's. 30 rooms plus a spacious roof
terrace. **£**

### COLUMBUS
*Via della Conciliazione 33*
*Tel: 686-5435*
Once a monastery on the wide, showy street
leading up to St Peter's. Still has fres-
coes and a walled garden. **£££**

## Via Veneto area

Still famous but mostly lacking its former glamour, it retains its old grand hotels, two of which are grand indeed.

### EXCELSIOR
*Via Veneto 125*
*Tel: 4708*
Nearly 400 extravagantly luxurious rooms,
imitation marble, silk-lined corridors and
abundant chandeliers all contribute to a
dramatic if slightly passé theatrical setting. **££££**

### MAJESTIC
*Via Veneto 50*
*Tel: 486-841*
Almost a century old, with a staggeringly
impressive guest-list including, in recent
years, Pavarotti, Stallone and Madonna.
An extravagant indulgence if you can af-
ford it. **££££**

*Seeing the sights*

## HEALTH & EMERGENCIES

All hospitals have a first aid department
which is free, so in case of unexpected
trouble or accident your best move is to
head for the nearest. A taxi to take you
there might well be faster than waiting
for an ambulance to arrive. The city's oldest hospital on the island in the Tiber
(tel: 587-3299) has been operating for
2,200 years.
There's an excellent private clinic in a

beautiful setting on top of the Gianicolo hill called the **Salvator Mundi** (Viale Mura Gianicolenei 67–77, tel: 586041). The staff here speak English and are fast, efficient and reliable. Go there if you can possibly afford it.

Pharmacies display the familiar red or green cross and can be found all over town. Quite a few offer homeopathic remedies. Telephone 1921 to ask for the ones open at night or just check the window of a closed pharmacy where details of the nearest one that's open will be posted.

For 24-hour medical assistance, tel: 47498 or (at night) 482-6741.

If you need emergency dental care, the Dental Centre Viminale (Via Palermo 28, tel: 484-863) has staff who speak English.

The various embassies can refer you to doctors who speak your language. They should be informed about loss of passports, money or valuables. Police buses with multilingual staff are situated at many points around the city.

Be wary of deft pickpockets and leave valuables at home or in the hotel safe. Don't allow colourful gypsy ladies and children to approach you with a piece of cardboard or newspaper extended. They try to crowd you, confuse you and pinch your valuables. Women's bags can be easily snatched by boys speeding past on motorcycles.

### Useful Telephone Numbers

**Police:** 113
**Police (Foreigners' Bureau):** 468-629
**Carabinieri** (almost a rival police organisation, with smarter uniforms): 112
**Traffic police:** 5544
**Ambulances:** 5100 (for Red Cross)
**Postal enquiries:** 180
**Directory enquiries:** 12
**Long distance:** 184

## COMMUNICATIONS & MEDIA

### Telephone

Here and there are telephones that still accept only coins (one 200-*lire* piece or two 100-*lire* coins) and occasionally you'll find phones that accept both coins and cards. But mostly you'll run across phones that accept only telephone cards, so be prepared. Tobacconists (identified with a big, black **T**) sell phone cards (L5,000 or L10,000) and also stamps and other useful items. As in other countries, hotels all too frequently add excessive surcharges for phone calls.

To dial other countries, first dial the outgoing code 00, then the country code: Australia (61), France (33), Germany (49), Japan (81), Netherlands (31), Spain (34), UK (44), US and Canada (1). If using a US credit phone card, dial the company's access number: Sprint, 172-1877; AT&T 172-1011; MCI, 172-1022.

### Postal Service

The main post office on Piazza San Silvestro is open until 9pm on weekdays and until noon on Saturdays. There are more than 100 branch offices, and these are open until 2pm. Stamps can be obtained at tobacconists bearing the **T** sign.

### Foreign Newspapers

All the big tourist spots have newsstands carrying foreign language papers and magazines, although London papers are more easily found than American ones (with the exception of *USA Today* and the *Wall Street*

*Journal*). The Paris edition of that day's *Herald Tribune* is usually available by midday. The two best kiosks in town are in the Via Veneto and remain open until 2am.

## What's On

Two English-language fortnightlies, *Wanted in Rome* (carrying info for all Italy) and *Metropolitan* (racier and focusing on the city) are available at newsstands. Also check out 'Trovaroma', a Thursday supplement to the daily *La Repubblica*.

## USEFUL INFORMATION

### Photography

Some museums and tourist sites impose a charge for taking photographs but only if they see your camera. Other museums including those of Vatican City ban photography altogether. Nobody is allowed to take pictures in the Sistine Chapel.

### The Pope

John Paul II's general audiences usually take place at 11am on Wednesdays in the audience chamber (November to February) or in the afternoon on St Peter's Square during the rest of the year. Requests for tickets can be made from the Prefetto della Casa Pontificia whose office is through the bronze door (Portone di Bronzo) at the right of the basilica. Tickets are issued on Tuesday and Wednesday mornings. On Sundays the pope gives a blessing from his study window over to the right-hand side of St Peter's Square. To visit the Vatican Gardens, apply at the office on the left of the square (tel: 698-4466) where most other questions concerning Vatican City can be answered.

During the summer the pope is often at Castel Gandolfo, in the Castelli hills south of Rome. (for information, call 9360340). In most bookstores you will find a fold-up poster called *I Sommi Pontefici Romani* ('The Roman Pontiffs') which lists in English (and Japanese on the reverse side) all 264 popes from St Peter to John Paul II (elected in 1978). Costing about £4, it contains a few lines about each pope – birthplace, background, date of election – and contains quite a few surprises in its small print.

## USEFUL ADDRESSES

### Tourist Information

Ente Provinciale per il Turismo, Via Parigi 5, near Termini station, is one option, but the CIT office at Piazza della Repubblica 68 tends to be more efficient. Best of all, acquire information from the tourist board before leaving your native country.

### Tourist Information Abroad

**Italian State Tourist Office:** 1 Princes Street, London W1R 8AY, tel: 0171-408 1254; fax: 493-6695.

**Italian Govt Tourist Office:** 630 Fifth Ave, New York 10111, tel: (212) 245-4822; fax: 586-9249.

### Consulates

**Australia**
Via Alessandra 215, tel: 832-2721.
**Britain**
Via XX Settembre 80a, tel: 834-194
**Canada**
Via Zara 30, tel: 844-1841.
**Ireland**
Largo Nazareno 3, tel: 678-2541
**USA**
Via Vittorio Veneto 121, tel: 46741

## FURTHER READING

*Insight Guide: Rome* (Apa Publications, 1994)
*D H Lawrence and Italy* (Viking Penguin, 1972)
*Rome: The Sweet Tempestuous Life* by Paul Hofman (Congdon & Weed, 1984)
*The Ides of March* by Thornton Wilder (Harper & Row, 1948)
*The Agony and the Ecstasy* by Irving Stone (Doubleday, 1961)

Index

# ACKNOWLEDGMENTS

| | |
|---|---|
| *Photography* | Frances Gransden *and* |
| *11, 48* | Ping Armand |
| *35, 41, 57, 81B* | Patrizia Giancotti |
| *32, 43, 54, 59, 61, 64, 67B, 75, 76T, 79,* | Elvira d'Ippoliti |
| *85, 87, 88, 89* | |
| *8/9, 58* | Jim Holmes |
| *12T, 12B* | Mary Evans Picture Library |
| *70,* | Gerd Pfeifer |
| *23, 29, 37, 46, 52, 56, 65, 67* | Mark Auriel Rettenbacher |
| *Production Editor* | Mohammed Dar |
| *Handwriting* | V Barl |
| *Cover Design* | Klaus Geisler |
| *Cartography* | Berndtson & Berndtson |